THE CLASSICAL GREEK HOUSE

'This book will make a major contribution to the study of the Greek oikos.'

> Lloyd Llewellyn-Jones, Senior Lecturer in
> Ancient History, University of Edinburgh

The Classical Greek House offers an illuminating reappraisal of domestic space in classical Greece. Beginning with a fresh evaluation of what 'home' meant to different communities in the ancient Greek world, Janett Morgan employs textual analysis alongside archaeological scholarship to explain some of the contradictions that previous approaches have left unanswered.

The text is supplemented by house plans and pictorial evidence, suggestions for further reading and a useful glossary.

Janett Morgan is lecturer in Greek Archaeology at Royal Holloway, University of London. She has published widely in classical studies; of particular note are her contributions to *Archaeology and Ancient History: Breaking the Boundaries* (2004) and *A Companion to Greek Religion* (2007).

Line drawing from an Attic salt cellar, c.540–530 BC.
The object on the far left is a house decorated for a wedding.
(Llewellyn-Jones 2003: Fig. 153)

THE CLASSICAL GREEK HOUSE

Janett Morgan

BRISTOL
PHOENIX
PRESS

Cover image: gravestone of Hegeso showing a domestic scene (author's image)

First published in 2010 by
Bristol Phoenix Press
an imprint of The Exeter Press
Reed Hall, Streatham Drive
Exeter EX4 4QR
UK
www.exeterpress.co.uk

British Library Cataloguing in Publication Data
A catalogue record for this book is available from the British Library.

Hardback ISBN 978 1 904675 74 7
Paperback ISBN 978 1 904675 75 4

Typeset in Chaparral Pro 11.5pt on 15pt
by JCS Publishing Services Ltd, www.jcs-publishing.co.uk

Printed in Great Britain by Short Run Press Ltd

CONTENTS

Illustrations

Frontispiece House decorated for a wedding

Figures

House plans (collected at the end of the text)

Acknowledgements

With thanks:

– To the Arts and Humanities Research Council and to Cardiff University Postgraduate Fund, whose financial contribution made my PhD research possible.

– To Nick Fisher, Ruth Westgate, Lin Foxhall and James Whitley who commented on the ideas used from my PhD.

– To the students on my Classical Cities course at Royal Holloway, University of London, whose comments helped me to clarify my ideas.

– To Lloyd Llewellyn-Jones and Shaun Tougher, who commented, frequently . . .

– To Bill and Joan Harrison, who now know far more than any normal person should about classical houses.

– To Robert, Charlotte and Alex who lived with it.

– To John Betts, sorely missed, who inspired it.

– To Simon Baker and Anna Henderson at University of Exeter Press for their hard work and invaluable advice.

A Note on the Text

I have used the original excavators' names for buildings at Athens, Halieis and for the buildings outside the grid system at Olynthus. For the many buildings discussed from inside the grid, I have simply used the reference number. My aim is to avoid confusion; the use of a name that includes the word 'House' does not imply that I agree with their identification of the building as domestic.

All translations from the Greek are my own. Where possible, line numbers for the Greek texts refer to the version on the Perseus website; the remainder refer to the appropriate Loeb edition.

GLOSSARY OF TERMS

---

agueia	an epithet of Apollo, referring to his presence in the streets
amphora	a two-handled vessel for carrying liquids such as wine, water or oil (plural: *amphorae*)
amphoriskos	a smaller version of an amphora
andreion	a Cretan military dining mess
andron	a men's room in classical texts
andronitis	men's quarters in classical texts
anoikismos	the removal of people from their original homes, mass migration
apothekes	storage pits
banausic	suitable only for craftsmen
bolsal	a type of drinking cup
bouleuterion	a public building that housed the council who ran the city
chernips	a vessel that held water for sprinkling on a ritual occasion
deme	a unit of territorial and political division in Athens
diaitateria	rooms for living in
domation	a small room or building
domos	a building
epinetron	a decorated ceramic knee protector for use in weaving or sewing

eschara   a fire for cooking on, or a brazier

gunaikon   a women's room in classical texts

gunaikonitis   women's quarters in classical texts

herm   a stone pillar with the head of the god Hermes

hestia   the goddess of the hearth or a fireplace

hiera   a shrine

hipnos   an oven or lantern

horos   a stone that marks a boundary, or a mortgage

katachysmata   a ceremony to join a bride or slave to a household, which involved the throwing of fertility symbols while the recipient sat at the hearth

kernos   a ritual vessel with many small cups attached to one stem

kopron   a pit for human waste

krater   a vessel for mixing wine and water

lebes gamikos   a vase made for weddings to carry water for the bride's bath

lekanis-pyxis   a small lidded box, usually associated with women

lekythos   a small oil flask

louter   a pedestal topped with a basin for holding water

melathron   a roofed building

metic   a non-Athenian who was given the right to live and work in Athens

muchos   a dark area, either a space within a room or room within a building

oecus   also called 'kitchen complex': a group of two or three rooms consisting of a hearth room (*oecus*), flue and bathroom

oikos	a building, room or all the possessions of a family
oinochoe	a vessel for pouring liquid
orgeones	a religious group that worshipped one deity
pastas	a covered porch area in a building
perirrhanterion	a vessel containing water, usually for washing
peristyle	a court consisting of central open space surrounded by four porch areas
phratry	a political and social organization in Athens
pithos	a storage vessel (plural: *pithoi*)
polis	an urban centre or land owned by an urban centre
prothyron	an entrance way to building, usually staggered to restrict visibility
protome	a mask of the head, shoulders and breasts for hanging on walls
prytaneion	a public building where the hearth of the city was kept and dining took place
pyxis	a small lidded box (plural: *pyxides*)
skyphos	a cup for drinking wine (plural: *skyphoi*)
stegos	a roofed place
stoa	a public building consisting of a covered porch with rooms at rear (plural: *stoai*)
strigil	a scraper to remove skin and sweat at washing or exercise
stylus	a writing implement
symposium	an all-male drinking party (plural: *symposia*)
synoikia	a property where rooms are leased by different tenants
synoikism	the joining together of communities to make a new community
thalamos	a private space or building

tholos   the round building that housed the *prytaneion* in Athens

triklinos   a room for three couches (plural: *triklina*)

INTRODUCTION

O n a bare hillside to the south of Athens lie the remains of a building called the Vari House. The Vari House had a relatively short lifespan, being both used and abandoned in the fourth century BC, yet its scattered and fragmentary remains offer us a glimpse into the lives of the people who used it. There are traces of burning on the floors, the residues of fires used for cooking and heating. Fragments of pottery from cooking pots, bowls and cups are strewn across the rooms, revealing that people ate and drank here. There are beehives, evidence of the production of honey at the site (Jones, Graham and Sackett 1973). The building is isolated, far from any settlement, and so the users must have been resident; in an age without cars, trains and bus services it would not have been feasible to live elsewhere and commute to this place on a daily basis. Set apart in their own small world, the users formed a discrete social group. They ate in the same building and slept in the same building; they lived and worked together. The users of the Vari House behaved as a unified residential group—a household—and so it is easy to see why the building has been identified as a house.

There must have been many rural dwellings like the Vari House dotted across the classical Greek countryside. Few survive. The Vari House offers us a unique chance to study a rural house and its household in detail; we can look at the presentation of rooms, at the relationships between rooms and at the artefacts present within them. Despite our apparently clear view of the Vari House in its splendid isolation, there is much that we will never know. We cannot see the identity of the inhabitants or understand their relationships with each other: we can only see the residues of their behaviour while they lived in the building. The isolation that allows us to view the house in detail also inhibits us from seeing its role as a functioning part of society. It stands alone—it can only tell us about itself. Yet houses are more than mere buildings: they exist in an ideological as well as physical sense. The way that people view, explain and construct their homes impacts on the organization of their houses and the relationship that develops between house and community. Ideas about family, economy and private or public life shape the domestic environment. One isolated rural house can tell us little about these matters. If we truly wish to learn more about the classical Greek house, we must look within the classical city. The cities of classical Greece offer us a wealth of domestic material. The size of cities and the number of houses needed to support their population means that we have many more examples of houses to study at urban sites. A contextual study of urban houses allows us to look at the house as a social phenomenon: we can examine how houses relate to each other and how they relate to the space of the city, as well as how they are used. This means that we can examine the house not only as a place of habitation but also as a symbolic canvas within the society that produced it. We can reintegrate the house into its social context and examine the contribution that the house made to political, religious and economic discourses in classical Greece.

In this book, we will consider the evidence for houses and the role of the house in three specific classical communities: Athens, Olynthus and Halieis (see **Fig. 1**). Each of these three communities offers us a very different perspective. They have different histories, they differ in their size, in geographical location and in the sources that they offer to our study. We will look not only at the architecture of the houses but also at the relationship between urban context and spatial arrangement. We will look at the shapes of houses and at the evidence for

1 *Map showing locations of Athens, Olynthus and Halieis (based on Nevett 1999: 54, Fig. 8)*

human activity in domestic spaces. We will look at the house as an ideological tool, as a social metaphor for the family and as a locus for different types of domestic behaviour. In doing this, we will gain a greater awareness of the important and different roles played by the house in the cities of classical Greece.

The silent houses of classical Greece

Despite the range and volume of domestic material available in our chosen classical cities, it is important to acknowledge from the outset that our view of the house will be neither direct nor clear. Our attempts to investigate will be hampered by the nature of our sources and by the contradictions between the views gained from texts and those gained from archaeology. Our ability to understand the evidence that we do find is limited further by the insidiousness of our own modern, cultural understanding of domesticity and our expectations of the domestic environment. Before we turn to examine the evidence, we will look in more detail at these problems, why they inhibit investigations, and at the approach we will take in seeking to negotiate them.

Our first problem is rooted in the sources that we use to investigate houses: texts and archaeology. The domestic context is difficult to access because material remains are disturbed and fragmentary and, as a result, cannot easily be understood. In cities, where the need for space is most pressing, private buildings took whatever space was available to them. Consequently, we cannot always tell where one building ends and another begins. They are vulnerable to processes of erosion and later human action, such as ploughing or rebuilding, at the site. This destroys walls and makes it difficult to see relationships between rooms. Artefacts are not always *in situ*: they can be dumped into wells, cisterns or rooms by householders as they abandon the property, or the artefacts can be moved by later human activity. We cannot be sure that we are viewing artefacts in their places of use: we could be looking at storage places or dumps of unwanted items (Foxhall 2000). Our understanding of the house might be based on household rubbish rather than important artefacts.

The archaeology at each of our three sites, Athens, Olynthus and Halieis, was shaped in different ways as a result of unique external factors. This affects the quality and quantity of material evidence available to us. At Athens, the city endured over time: houses rose and fell, their remains were built over, time and time again. Houses in use during the fifth and fourth centuries BC, the classical era, were buried under the buildings of later generations. Artefacts were abandoned as the householders moved on and properties were cleared; there is precious little on the house floors to allow us to look at room use or domestic behaviour. This contrasts with the evidence from Olynthus, which is almost entirely archaeological. Most of the houses here were constructed in the fifth century BC and abandoned as the troops of Philip of Macedon approached in around 348 BC. Although the city was looted and buildings burned, the site was not built over. The foundations of many of the houses remain and there are artefacts on the house floors and inscriptions from mortgages and house sales which offer potential insights into the lives of the residents. At Halieis, the city was slowly abandoned through the late fourth and early third century BC, after years of being a political pawn in the military struggles of more powerful Peloponnesian neighbours. The foundations of the houses are visible, but it is difficult to identify clearly the divisions between them. Artefacts are present, although these are mostly dumped in cisterns or heaped in rooms, which suggests that they are refuse, abandoned when the inhabitants left. Our ability to read the material evidence is complicated by the unique histories of each site.

In the absence of a clear archaeological perspective, we can turn to classical texts to enhance our understanding of classical houses. Yet, while texts offer us abundant information about human behaviour, our ability to view or study houses through texts is also limited. Unlike modern western society, where magazines offer us guided tours of celebrities' houses and novels present insights into domestic disharmony and domestic behaviour, for the classical Greeks, private meant private. There is no genre of domestic literature—we have no direct view of the classical house and its residents. We obtain our impressions from excerpts that are incidental to wider narratives or derived from fantastic situations. We try to understand life in the classical Greek house from studying the domestic behaviour of royal families in tragedies or the ideological descriptions of philosophers. The arrangements in each of these cases are serving the needs of the author and narrative rather than offering a true reflection of private life in a classical Greek household. We must be careful when using classical texts as evidence for private behaviour. We would not expect to fully understand domestic life in rural 1950s England by studying *The Lord of the Rings*, even though many households are described in it.

Even where texts offer us clear views of houses or domestic behaviour, the oblique perspective of our information means that we cannot read it as a literal representation. While pleading in his defence before a classical Athenian jury, the citizen Euphiletos tells them: 'And so first, gentlemen . . . my little house is on two floors with the upper being equal to the lower, with the women's space above and men's below' (Lysias 1.9). Euphiletos' house is that of a fine, upstanding citizen. His arrangement of domestic space appears straightforward: the division of the domestic space into male and female areas is set out as normal practice. Yet Euphiletos has a hidden agenda, he is using his house as a symbol to show the jury that he is a good citizen. He wants them to know not only that he owns property in Athens—a right limited to Athenian citizens—but also that he leads a well-ordered life. So, how should we understand the information here? Is Euphiletos describing a real situation or creating a false façade of respectability in front of the jury? We must retain an awareness of the needs of the narrative and its effect on the presentation of house and household life.

Can we make the houses speak?

Our ability to read classical texts and archaeology is further inhibited by the choices that we make in seeking to use them. As our sources are fragmentary, we tend to group them together; we add Athenian texts to Olynthian material remains to create a single narrative for classical domesticity—to make the silent houses speak. We take information about the role of the household hearth from texts and we illustrate our narrative using images of hearths from Olynthus. This approach fails for two vital reasons. First, in combining texts and material evidence we fail to pay sufficient attention to the fact that the vast majority of classical texts come from Athens. They describe Athenian people, Athenian places and Athenian behaviour. We know that the cities of Greece had very different political and religious practices yet we assume that their domestic practices were identical to the practices of the Athenian household. We read all houses through the filter of Athenian life, ignoring the possibility that there may be regional differences in the relationship between houses and their community. The second problem lies in the assumption that we can create a single narrative for classical domesticity. In combining our sources we ignore the truth that the views offered by texts and archaeology are not the same; in fact, they contradict each other. Certain features that appear to be essential in texts, such as the separate rooms for women in Euphiletos' house, are noticeably absent in the ruins of classical houses.

Archaeologists such as Michael Jameson and Lisa Nevett argue that material evidence should be examined in context and treated as a single, unique source, not simply used as a means to illustrate texts (Jameson 1990; Nevett 1999). They suggest that the differences between text and archaeology are too great—they cannot be woven together to create a composite picture. Features that appear in texts do not appear in houses; texts cannot explain the spatial arrangements of the classical Greek house. Archaeology and texts, archaeologists and classicists cannot agree on the presentation and use of the house in classical Greece: their source-based perspectives offer very different views. It is not just the privacy of the domestic context that prevents research but a stalemate between scholars over the best way to use the evidence.

So, who is right, archaeologists or classicists? Why do classical texts and archaeology not only disagree but also contradict each other in their presentations of houses? As we have already noted, the root of the problem lies in the fact that the classical house exists as an ideological tool and as a physical location. When Euphiletos tells us that his house had an area set aside for the exclusive use of women, he is creating an image of himself as a man who behaves in an orderly manner. This implies that he behaved reasonably in the killing of Eratosthenes, who entered his house and committed adultery with his wife. Euphiletos' words are designed to strike a chord with the jury: he is one of them, a decent citizen. He is not setting out a blueprint for the physical structure of all classical Greek or even Athenian houses. Texts tell us that the hearth was a vital component of religious life in the household, yet only one hearth has been identified in the material remains of Athenian houses—hardly an essential domestic feature. Therefore is the hearth more of an ideological construction, a means to describe the shared blood links between family members rather than a practical reality? Instead of focusing on the contradictions and using them as an excuse to separate texts and material remains, we should ask ourselves why is there no convergence between our sources, and how far the fault lies in our expectations of the evidence rather than in the evidence itself.

In this study we will take a contextual approach and examine the evidence from our three sites separately. Each chapter will begin with Athens and look at the information that texts and archaeology can reveal about the role of the house here. Texts can tell us about the appearance of the house as well as the residents and the way that they lived their lives. Texts can also show us the role of the house in gender, social, political and religious ideology. Yet these topics are not the exclusive preserve of texts: ideas about social behaviour and political ideology can be encoded into domestic and urban architecture. We will therefore compare and contrast the perspectives offered by Athenian texts and material evidence, allowing them to reinforce or contradict ideas from each other and offer us a more nuanced view of the role of the house in Athenian society. We will then investigate Olynthus and Halieis. At both of these sites, our evidence is material rather than textual and so we will compare this evidence with material evidence from Athens. We will look for areas of similarity and difference and consider what we can learn from these about the symbolic and practical roles of the house in these two communities.

Cultural contradictions

One of the greatest problems in the way that we investigate and explain classical houses is the dominance of our own cultural perspective. We cannot escape our own contemporary cultural beliefs about domesticity—indeed, we expect to see our beliefs reflected in the ancient remains. We have an idea, an expectation, of how a house should look, what features it needs and how its spaces were used. In 1938, when the excavators Robinson and Graham drew a model plan of the houses at Olynthus, they sought to classify the architecture, to seek the functions of rooms and through them to explain spatial use in the house. They identified rooms as living rooms, kitchens and bathrooms (Robinson and Graham 1938). This is dangerous. When we use modern terms to describe ancient houses, we force the reader to make an assumption about what kind of artefacts would be in the room and what kind of behaviour took place there. We also reinforce the idea that each house is the location of a single family, and describe the house as directly reflecting their needs: each building is labelled as containing one bathroom and one kitchen. This reflects the modern western understanding of domesticity, where families fragment on marriage and create a new, replica house. The pattern of social fragmentation and replicated habitation is undermined if we look more closely at the textual evidence from Athens. Here we find stories of different generations of a family living together. In the law court speech 'Against Simon', the speaker reveals that he shares a house with his sister and his nieces; in 'On the Murder of Eratosthenes', the husband Euphiletos tells the court how, after marriage, his new wife came into his family home (Lysias 3.6; Lysias 1.6). Descriptions of the households involved in the case 'Against Boeotus' (Demosthenes 39 and 40) show that second or even third marriages could produce complex arrangements of close and distant family members sharing property (Gallant 1991: 24–5).

While these speeches may reflect short-term arrangements, they raise the possibility that our reconstruction of spatial use and users in the classical house may be masking a more complicated picture. Why should we assume that modern western houses are a suitable model for family and space in the classical Greek house? In modern Iran, a house can be a few rooms in a larger building inhabited by a family group (Kramer 1982). In Japan, a house can be a large space that is subdivided by temporary screens, so that its 'rooms' can alter according to changes in time and the needs of the family (Bognar 1989). For the Masai tribesmen, home is the shelter where the family settles for the night, the location or its permanence is irrelevant. The communities in these examples all see their space as a house—as their home—yet the physical appearance of the building clearly will not match the blueprint for the modern western house. Houses are not the same in all cultures. In classical Greek cities a number of families may have shared the same building: each private building may have been the location of several 'houses' and households. In view of this, can we be sure that we have correctly identified buildings as houses?

In order to deal with the pervasive influence of cultural expectation, we will explicitly examine the ideas about the house and city that exist in modern western society. In each chapter, we will look at the modern beliefs relating to our discussion topic. We will examine our cultural expectations before approaching the ancient evidence and, in doing so, consider how they might affect our interpretation of the ancient evidence and seek to avoid imposing them onto the material remains.

Re-viewing the classical Greek house

The long litany of difficulties we face makes our task of understanding the role of the house in the classical Greek community seem a daunting one. Yet the problems are not insurmountable. As long as we maintain a healthy degree of caution, there is no bar to our ability to explore material and textual evidence. The presence of children's toys in a room may reflect a place of storage rather than a place of use, but we can still use it to discuss the role of the house as a family space. While one loom weight tells us nothing, loom weights found together with a mirror, a *pyxis* and jewellery could be indicative of a female presence, even if it is not at that precise spot. We must acknowledge differences in the material evidence between sites and look at what we can learn from them rather than seek to find a model to explain all classical houses in all Greek communities. We may compare evidence between sites but we must not seek to use one site as a model for another.

We will not be looking at the Vari House. A single, isolated residence is easier to study but can tell us little about the role of the house in classical Greece. This book will not seek to classify the house as a prerequisite to explaining its spatial arrangement. Instead, we will look for evidence of the different roles that houses play in urban political, social, economic, ideological and gender discourses. We will begin by considering the house as a built environment, looking at the place of the house in the political and religious life of the community and at how its appearance, use and ideology were affected by and impacted on the wider life of the city. We will then move to consider the house as a social environment, looking at the evidence for habitation in buildings. What can texts and material evidence tell us about the users of private buildings? Can we identify families in material remains?

The economic role of the household will provide the basis for our third investigation. In this section we will look at the evidence for manufacture and production in private contexts and consider the relationship between the urban economy and its houses. Next we will focus on the role of the house as an ideological and practical setting for gender relations. In particular, we will consider the relationship between gender separation and domestic architecture. Finally, we will look at the house as a religious site. What evidence do we have for domestic religious behaviour and what can this tell us about the practice of cult in house and city? Our aims in each of these investigations are to explore the role of the house as an essential component of urban space in a physical and ideological sense, to consider the effect of its symbolic and practical roles on the presentation and use of the house; by doing this, the aim is to increase our understanding of the role of the classical Greek house as an integral and unique feature of the society that produced it.

CHAPTER 1

HOUSE AND CITY,
PUBLIC AND PRIVATE
THE URBAN LANDSCAPE

We begin our investigations by looking at the organization of urban space within Athens, Olynthus and Halieis and at the place of the house within the city. All social groups construct their own communities; in doing so, they design and create a built environment that facilitates and also expresses the political, commercial, religious and private activities that are a natural part of life within their city. One of the clearest examples of the relationship between urban organization and human society can be seen in the American and British cities constructed in the nineteenth century and in the period after the Second World War. Here, urban plans were designed to create an 'ideal' environment, one that integrated the needs of residents with the commercial and economic activities necessary to urban life. The New York State Commissioners' Plan of 1811 used a grid to organize urban space in Manhattan: avenues, running north to south, were bisected by streets running east to west, creating blocks; urban activities—such as habitation, commerce and finance—became dominant in certain blocks, creating discrete zones. In the 'new towns' of post-war Britain, such as Milton Keynes and Stevenage, regular street patterns created similarly self-contained neighbourhoods, each consisting predominantly of housing but with their own central zone with local shops and local amenities. Industrial estates were located on the edges of the new towns. As a result, when we look at cities in the USA and the UK, we see patterns in architectural design and layout that inform us about the use of urban space.

Within these 'new' cities, the form and location of buildings reinforces and emphasizes the connection between human behaviour and the organization of the built environment. Shops have an open aspect and face onto the street to entice the passer-by; they are often grouped into a commercial district, located near to the centre of the city or at the centre of the neighbourhood. Factories, with their large floor space, can be found at the margins of the community, where they can utilize the more open areas of land and cause least disturbance. Public buildings can be recognized by their expensive building materials and decoration; they are often located in the oldest parts of the city or in its central areas. Religious buildings, identifiable by their unique architecture, are distributed through the city; each is located in a manner designed to allow it to cater for the needs of the people living in a particular district. Houses are woven through the city in small enclaves or gathered together at the edges of it in suburbs. Housing zones are clearly recognizable through the buildings' repetition of shape, size and layout. These examples reveal and express our deeply held view that politics, the workplace and the home are separate spheres of activity that should be kept apart in urban life. This is not only a physical matter but also an expression of ideology: the house is private space, the city is public space. A study of the spatial organization of new cities demonstrates how a modern community structures its urban world and reveals the social ideologies that underpin life in that community.

The organized shape of the new towns was an expression of the post-war desire for harmony. They were concrete utopias where the lives of the inhabitants and their needs and social beliefs were clearly woven into the urban structure; they followed an 'ideal' pattern of urban spatial use. We do not necessarily find this pattern in all cities in the USA and UK, but it best expresses contemporary thought in these countries of what a city should look like and how it should be used. An ideal plan could be constructed because society in both the USA and the UK was discrete and unified, their citizens shared common goals, common attitudes and had a common political organization within the country. It is important to remember that national unity was not present within classical Greece; it was only under the threat of the Persian invasion that the communities of Greece joined forces. Even then, some communities such as Thebes chose not to join in the united defence. The communities of classical Greece were separate and distinct. They had different political systems and different rules about citizenship and they worshipped different gods. This poses questions about urban organization in classical cities. It is possible that we will not find one clear model of urban planning in our three cities; it is highly unlikely that we will find an arrangement that mirrors the needs and beliefs of more modern cities. A contextual study of houses in their communities offers us an opportunity to explore the unique role of the house as a feature, product and expression of urban life at that site. So what can a study of houses in their urban context tell us about the role of the house in Athens, Olynthus and Halieis?

House and city in Athens: a material perspective

Texts from classical Athens name a wide range of buildings and activities that were located within the city. We have descriptions of political and administrative behaviour, with boards of magistrates meeting in the spaces of the Agora, the *demos* voting in the Pnyx and juries working in the law courts (Aristotle *Constitution of Athens* 42–69). Tales of religious festivals, sacrifices and cult dining thread through the narratives of comic and tragic plays as well as appearing in philosophical tracts and public inscriptions (Aristophanes *Acharnians* 237–79; Xenophon *Symposium* 1.1–4). We can read about buyers and sellers in the Agora and even learn about those who engaged in trade and industrial activity (Xenophon *Revenues* 5.3–4). There are also references to families and to the family home (Lysias 1.6–10). Life is complex, with clear religious, commercial, political and social dimensions that might be reflected in the urban layout.

The first area where we find a significant difference between classical Athens and modern cities is in the treatment of religious structures. While religious buildings are distributed in the modern city according to the needs of neighbourhoods, in Athens we can identify a specific religious zone. The temples and shrines on the Athenian Acropolis make a clear statement about the type of actions performed there and about the sanctity of the whole area. The geography of the Acropolis sets this area aside, raising it above the city and making it exclusive in function (see **Fig. 2**). Despite the clear separation of this area, we cannot say that religious activity is zoned: temples, shrines and altars litter the streets of the city, but do not appear to correspond to specific districts and there is no rhyme or reason apparent for their placement. This reflects a very different attitude to religion. Rather than being controlled entirely by the state or by a religious organization following a single doctrine, religion in Athens was also an individual enterprise. Religious sites—temples, altars and shrines—were set up by small cult groups or by individual donors for the use of all. The result is that religious space was woven into political space and secular space; there is no clear division between religion and other urban activities and no evidence of a city blueprint that regulated the locations of religious constructions.

In contrast with this, it is easier to see the area of the Athenian Agora as a designated commercial or public zone. Houses were cleared from its central, western and southern sections in the late sixth century BC in order to allow the area to be developed as a public space. There are buildings that relate to the constitution of the city, including the Bouleuterion, where the Council met, and law courts such as the Heliaia. Scholars also see the Athenian Agora as the commercial heart of the city and there is evidence to support this from archaeology as well as texts. In the *Constitution of Athens* (51.1) Aristotle sets out details of the various magistrates who control markets, weights and measures

2   *Athenian Acropolis overlooking the Agora (photo J.E. Morgan)*

and contracts, and he locates them in the Agora. The shape of
the Agora—with its open spaces and borders marked by *stoai*—
is well suited to the establishment of stalls or to the hiring of
rooms in a *stoa* for buying and selling goods. Excavations in the
stoai surrounding the Agora found weights and measures, and
some of the rooms in the South Stoa contained coins, suggesting
that its rooms had been used as shops (Thompson 1968). In the
north of the Agora, the Classical Commercial Building contained
discarded pottery and terracotta figurines that had been offered
for sale there (Camp 1999). Yet, the Agora was not an exclusively
public or commercial space. Religious activity and religious
spaces wove through the area: the Altar of the Twelve Gods was
constructed in the north-west corner and the South Stoa housed
a shrine, placed outside a dining room that may have been used
for cult activities. The area of the Agora was bounded by temples
and shrines; the Agora itself was seen as a sacred space. There is
also evidence of residence and industrial activity there. At the
edges of the Agora, buildings such as the House of Mikion and
Menon contained evidence of residence. The House of Simon
in the south-west corner was a home as well as a cobbler's
workshop. An industrial building, the Mint, was placed in the
south-east corner. Although there is a great deal of commercial
and public evidence here, these are not the only activities that
we find. In the Athenian Agora, religion, politics, commerce and
habitation mingle.

A lack of regulation is also apparent in the distribution of
'industrial' areas. The buildings located in the valley between
the Areopagus and the Hill of the Nymphs contained evidence
of many different heavy trades such as marble working, bronze
casting and even dyeing, which resulted in the excavator naming
the area the 'Industrial District' (Young 1951). In the Street of
the Marble Workers the remains of around thirteen buildings

have been identified that were in use during the fifth and fourth centuries BC. House D contained a large hearth with evidence of metalworking (see **Plan 2**, p. 174). House F had three vats lined with waterproof cement, indicating that the occupiers were working with or soaking material in liquid. An establishment to the north of House F also had a large waterproof cement tank, the sides of which had a glassy granular substance, the residue of a manufacturing process. Yet this is not an exclusively industrial zone, there are small shrines in the streets and, although the buildings in the Street of the Marble Workers were littered with chips of marble—showing that marble working took place here—there is also evidence that the buildings were lived in. Evidence of production also spreads out across the city. A house on the north-east slopes of the Areopagus had a stucco-lined tank similar to those in the Street of the Marble Workers (see **Plan 1**, p. 173). The remains of a potter's establishment was uncovered beneath the eastern edge of the Panathenaic Way in the north-west of the Agora. Another potter's establishment was destroyed and covered over by the construction of the Stoa of Zeus on the Kolonos Agoraios, while a concentration of coroplasts' clay moulds and plaques were found in the remains on the north and west slopes of the Areopagus. It is a confusing and confused picture. There appears to have been little effort to regulate the way that the spaces of the city were used. Religion, habitation and industrial production all merge together and spread throughout classical Athens.

What can we learn from this? First, there may be a number of very practical reasons for this impression of integration in urban activities. Industrial activity was practised on a much smaller scale than in modern cities, and was in the control of individuals or families rather than state or business organizations. As a result, there were no large-scale factories. Industry, production and commerce did not need large buildings or zoned activity areas; they could integrate in the spaces of the city, alongside the houses. Secondly, the lack of activity zones may also reflect the antiquity of the city. Athens had existed as a settlement for a very long time: there are fragments of Mycenaean buildings on the Acropolis and Iron Age dedications and archaic cemeteries lie buried under the remains of classical buildings. The city had developed in a piecemeal manner over a long period; it had not been laid down quickly or with forethought and planned as in some of the cities rebuilt in the classical period, such as Rhodes, or as in the new modern cities that we examined at the start of this chapter. As a result, activities such as residence fitted into the city's development rather than being placed in a neatly predetermined area. In a city the size of Athens, where space was at a premium, users found a place for their activities wherever they could. Thirdly, the integration of activity spaces in Athens may reflect different ideas about the role and use of urban space. In Athens, the places of gods and political administration are set apart by their monumental structure: they use expensive materials such as stone and marble, they are decorated and, as a result, stand out clearly from their surroundings. Their visibility reveals their importance in urban life. We know that there were many people working and living in the city, yet material evidence does not allow us to identify residential areas clearly—they do not need to be separated or monumentalized. Apart from the central area with the Agora and its monumental buildings and the Acropolis with its religious buildings, there is no clear differentiation between industrial and residential, between commercial and religious buildings. The streets of Athens are awash with every type of activity. This appears to suggest that Athenians saw no reason to separate private activities from urban activities; they were all part of the ingredients of city life.

Urban ideology and urban space at Athens

Textual evidence from Athens reinforces the impression we gain from material evidence of its blurring of boundaries between activities and spaces. Texts constantly emphasize the importance of unity and the mutual dependence between resident and community; their success or failure is intimately entwined. This notion forms an explicit component of plays such as Sophocles' *Antigone* and the *Oresteia* trilogy of Aeschylus. In the final part of the *Oresteia* trilogy, the *Eumenides*, the cycle of family murder and bloodshed is only ended when Orestes is tried by the city of Athens and acquitted. The family must accept the justice of the city if the community is to survive. In *Antigone*, the eponymous heroine steps outside the city and its laws—in a literal and metaphorical sense—to administer death rites to the corpse of her brother, actions that spark a conflict between household and city. The play offers a warning that the city must not be allowed to override the rights of families. Without co-operation both family and city will fail.

The plays do not necessarily reflect a real conflict, but they act as a reminder of the importance of balancing the needs of house and city in Athens. In order to maintain social cohesion, households needed reminding of their role within the community and their importance to it. In Athens, the relationship between house and city was explored and reinforced by participation in the numerous community festivals that in subtle and not so subtle ways sought to map the land of the community, to identify the groups of people that lived there and to tie the people of the city into a common ritual landscape. Many of these festivals involved the participation of members of the household in individual capacities. At the Panathenaia, almost all of the different groups that lived in the city—*metics*, young girls, magistrates and cavalrymen—were represented in the procession from the Kerameikos up the Sacred Way to the Parthenon. Our evidence for this great occasion comes from a wide range of sources (Neils 1992). We see a depiction of this procession in the Parthenon Frieze and in the descriptions of competitors, events and administration found in inscriptions and texts (Aristophanes *Frogs* 1087–95; Aristotle *Constitution of Athens* 60.3). In the Panathenaic procession, the different social groups that made up the Athenian population marched in unity across their city to worship their goddess. It was a powerful and symbolic act—whatever their place in the Athenian social system, they were a united community.

Athenian festivals did not focus solely on the land of the city but also used the space of the house as an essential part of their rites. During the three-day Anthesteria festival in the month of Anthesterion, the location of ritual action fluctuated between the sanctuary and the house. On the first day (Pithoigia) new jars of wine were opened to honour the god Dionysus at his sanctuary. On the second day (Choes) the sanctuary was closed off and ritual events took place at the house. The house door was painted with pitch to protect it from the ghosts that were believed to walk the city at this time; the painting of the door sealed the house, effectively separating it from the community. The residents indulged in drinking rituals in a family rather than a social or public context. On day three (Chytra) the household re-entered the community and there was a public drinking competition during which participants ate dishes of grains and honey. Although the Anthesteria is ostensibly concerned with spring and new wine, the role of the house is essential. In this festival the community fragments into separate houses only to rejoin or reform at the end. Without the community there is only isolation, darkness and fear; with the community comes sociability and fun. The festival and its use of private and public space illustrate the benefits of urban life and the mutual dependence of house and city.

The relationship between house and city was also explored in exclusively female festivals. At the Thesmophoria, citizen wives left the household, separating themselves from their husbands and families. They celebrated together in the public spaces of the city, making sacrifices, handling sacred artefacts and laughing, blaspheming or abusing each other (Dillon 2002). Texts directly associate women's lives with the family home to the extent that the wife herself can symbolize the home; Euphiletos equates the sexual penetration of his wife by Eratosthenes with the latter's illicit entry into his house (Lysias 1.4). Bearing this in mind, we can see that the movement of the wife out of the house and into the political places of the city symbolically dissolved spatial and gender boundaries: the city became a house as the women occupied the political sphere. The festival of the Adonia also integrated social and spatial activity. At this festival, all women, whether maiden or mother, citizen wife or prostitute, could participate. In honour of the god Adonis the participants grew gardens that were placed on the roof of the house, where they withered and died in the heat (Plato *Phaedrus* 276B). The female participants also feasted, danced and shouted on the roofs of their houses (Aristophanes *Lysistrata* 387–96) and were possessed by their grief—their vulnerability derived from their state of religious ecstasy. The roof offered a space that was visible and yet protected. They could behave in a way that would not generally be considered appropriate for women: drinking, making noise and losing their self-control, yet they retained the protection of the home. By using the roof of the house, the women became visible and audible without coming out into the city; they were protected and avoided taking their ritual and physical vulnerability into public spaces. In a sense, the festival came to them. The female festivals give us an image of integration rather than separation; ideological boundaries between men and women and between city and household are broken down to allow society to reflect on the roles of its occupants and to reconstitute itself. This reinforces the view of the mixing of activities that is shown by a study of urban archaeology in Athens.

House and city: Athenian private rites

The mutual dependence of house and city was reinforced not only by public festivals but also by private ritual occasions. Rituals performed at births, deaths and marriages articulated and recorded changes in the composition of the household, and as such they were the most prominent and visible of all domestic rites. These life stages changed the composition of both the citizen body and also the household unit. Their importance to both is reflected in the pattern of ritual behaviour that we find in texts. The three occasions followed a similar ritual structure that used public and private spaces to advertise, reinforce and integrate the private changes into the ritual landscape of the community.

In the first stage the household made public offerings in anticipation of the changes that would occur. The city wanted successful marriages and a supply of babies to be citizens, a need that is reflected in the geo-political landscape of the city. The community provided the sanctuary; the family brought the gifts. At birth and marriage, families made offerings in public shrines and sanctuaries for the safe passage of the bride or mother through the rites and in hope of a successful outcome (Euripides *Hippolytus* 1425–7; Euripides *Iphigenia in Aulis* 433–39; Aristotle *Politics* 7.1335B). The use of the public setting acknowledged the vulnerability of household and city and their shared interest in the protection of female fertility (Demand 1994). By coming out of the house and placing personal gifts in a public setting, the family drew attention to itself in a very public advertisement for the changes that were to take place.

The second stage of the process focused directly on the house as it was symbolically separated from the community. A passage from *Alcestis* offers evidence for the way that the house was marked and separated from the community when death occurred in the family (Euripides *Alcestis* 98–104). The chorus of citizens of Pherae look for a water vessel and a lock of hair placed at the entrance of the house, and they listen for the sound of women lamenting. Similarly, at weddings, the house was marked out as a ritual place by decorating it with ribbons and foliage (Oakley and Sinos 1993). An example of this decoration can be seen in the wedding scene on an Attic salt cellar which shows the whole house with foliage wrapped around it (see Frontispiece). There was also the sound of women singing; in *Phaethon* the chorus of girls is told to sing and dance around the rooms of the palace and the places of the gods within it (Euripides *Phaethon* 245–50). The marking of the house at birth was equally clear. It was sufficiently visible that the Superstitious Man can avoid places of death and birth (Theophrastus *Characters* 16.9).

The marking of the house was symbolic as well as decorative. In the public sphere, *louters* or water vessels were placed at the edges of sanctuaries; they divided the spaces of men from the spaces of gods. At the house of the deceased, the placement of a water vessel at the main door may also have indicated a division in space between the city and the place where ritual was dominant, albeit temporarily. The markings at weddings and birth offered protection to the vulnerable bride or mother and baby as well as acting as a sign of events inside. The family withdrew behind the symbolic boundary into their house and stopped participating in the life of the city. This is an interesting paradox: when the house withdrew from the community and separated itself it became highly visible. Through the symbolic marking of the house and the noise within it, the behaviour of the family was brought to the attention of the whole community and the house was set apart by its visibility.

Having marked the house as a separate unit within the community, the body of the individual undergoing the transition was purified and adorned. The bride was ritually bathed in water from a source renowned for its sacred nature or especial purity (Thucydides 2.15.5; Aristophanes *Peace* 842–3, 868; Euripides *Iphigenia in Tauris* 818). The body of the deceased was also washed and purified (Euripides *Hecuba* 609–13). Having been purified, bride and corpse were adorned in elaborate robes. These acts were of great symbolic importance as they ensured that the individual was firmly placed as the focus of attention and at the centre of the rites. Their clothes and crowns separated them in a visual sense from the family around them.

A unique and separate space, marked by artefacts and human bodies, was then created for the central individual within the house. Aristophanes described how the deceased was crowned, oregano strewn over him and vine twigs placed under him, he was bound with a ribbon and a *lekythos* or oil flask was placed beside him (Aristophanes *Assembly Women* 535–8, 1030–3). The mother and an area within the birth chamber might be purified with water, and amulets or protective plants used to mark the birth-space (Aristophanes *Women at the Thesmophoria* 504). The individual at the focus of the ritual was also 'attended' by particular people. On marriage, the bride was looked after by a group of her friends; at births, the group consisted of mature women; on death, the closest relatives surrounded the body, with women placed at the head and men at the feet, forming a circle that enclosed the corpse (Shapiro 1991). The participants moved and made noise, which might be singing, lamenting or incanting, depending on the occasion (Sophocles *Electra* 750; Euripides *Medea* 1172–7; Plato *Theaetetus* 149D).

What we see here is a reverse telescope effect. We begin in the wider community, turn to focus on the house and then, in our next stage, focus in on the body of the individual undergoing the rite of transition. These were the three most important components of the Athenian community: its wider body, its houses or households and the individuals within them. We are in effect breaking the community down into its essential building blocks and marking the space of each during the process of the rite.

The next stage involved physical change, which complemented the social and ritual change. This occured through formal rites of movement. The bride or corpse and their family came out of the house into the streets of the city and the individual at the centre of the rites was escorted to their new place of residence. The corpse was taken to its new space outside the city, in the graveyard (Demosthenes 43.62; Thucydides 2.34; Plato *Laws* 959E–960A); the bride was taken to her new home (Euripides *Suppliant Maidens* 990–1000; *Helen* 724–5). Although the procession walked the streets of the city, this was no community act—participation at rites of transition stripped the family to its essential members and separated them from the city. Their separation was enhanced by the time of the procession— twilight is liminal, neither day nor night—and by the use of fire. Vases of the wedding procession clearly show the presence of torchbearers in front of and behind the bride (Oakley and Sinos 1993). The torches created a purified space around the bride, sanctifying her route in the same way as torches purified the passage of public processions. The procession protected the corpse and bride because they were between states in the human life cycle and so believed to be vulnerable. The procession moved through the community but at this moment its members were not a functioning part of the community. It was a statement of family, made within a public setting.

At birth the movement was not of household into city but of goddess into house. In order to come to the house, the goddess had to be called, and a clear depiction of this call can be seen in *Hippolytus*, where the nurse states: 'And I called out to the one who cares for and helps in childbirth, heavenly Artemis of arrows' (Euripides *Hippolytus* 166–8). The goddess was not perceived as being a permanent part of domestic space. Her place was in the public world, where offerings could be made before or after birth. She was called to the side of the woman in labour to deliver the baby safely and then returned to her temple immediately afterwards to wait for offerings of gratitude.

Once individuals attained their new places within the household, the restoration of the community could take place as the individual and their families were reintegrated into society. Again, the house played a central role: following the completion of rites for the corpse, the family of the deceased returned to the house for the funeral feast, which took into account the changed structure of the family (Demosthenes 18.288). On arrival at her new house the bride participated in a ritual called the *katachysmata*, which joined outsiders to the family. The new members—whether slave or bride and groom—sat at the hearth and were showered with fruits and seeds, symbols of wealth and fertility (Demosthenes 45.74; Aristophanes *Wealth* 768). There were also ceremonies in the house to introduce the new baby to its wider family, occasions that were often used in legal cases as proof of legitimacy (Isaeus 3.70–1; Demosthenes 40.59). The

door of the house was hung with symbols that signified a successful birth as well as the gender of the baby: an olive branch for
a boy and wool for a girl (Hesychius *s.v.* 'Stephanon Ekpherein').
An allotted period of separation was served until the ritual
pollution was deemed to have passed and the house was then
purified. The restrictions on the house were now removed, its
space was no longer marked and the family and house re-entered
the community.

In both public and private festivals at Athens we see the
house used as a physical location and, more importantly, as an
ideological tool to express the need to integrate the houses and
public areas of the city, to reflect the need for mutual dependence
between household and community. A study of Athenian rituals
emphasizes the importance of integration between public and
private spheres of activity in the city. This may be a reflected in
the material evidence and the difficulties that we have in viewing
specific activity zones within classical Athens.

Residence at Olynthus

We turn now to Olynthus in northern Greece. The city is
located across a plateau that spreads over two hills, the South
Hill and the North Hill. While there are some signs of Neolithic
habitation, clear evidence of a constructed settlement can be
found on the South Hill from the seventh century BC onwards.
The area of the South Hill is around seven hectares (7,000m^2)
and Cahill estimates that it held 1,050 people (2002: 38). The
area contains fragmentary evidence of streets and walls but
it is difficult to see relationships between buildings or even to
identify where one building begins and another ends. In contrast
with the haphazard organization of the South Hill, the North
Hill at Olynthus appears to be a model of regular planning. The

3 Houses from the grid system on the North Hill at Olynthus
(photo J.E. Morgan)

area is approximately twenty-eight hectares (28,000m^2) and is
dominated by regular rows of similarly sized buildings set into a
grid pattern (see **Fig. 3**).

In 432 BC the coastal settlements in the neighbourhood of
Olynthus were abandoned and the inhabitants moved inland
to Olynthus. It is thought to have been at this time that the
developments on the North Hill and East Spur Hill were built.
All scholars are generally agreed that the construction of
buildings here dates to the *anoikismos* of 432 BC, mentioned by
Thucydides (1.58–9). The construction on the North Hill was
planned in advance; it was a new settlement, designed to hold
a new community and, unlike the settlement on the South Hill
and in Athens, there was an opportunity to think about how

space should be organized. The North Hill offers us an unrivalled opportunity to investigate what the planners saw as essential features in their community and how they arranged that space.

All communities require some degree of central organization and, as our study of Athens showed, public administrative buildings and religious buildings stand out from others due to their size, materials and decoration. So, what can the administrative and religious buildings of Olynthus tell us about the community there? The excavator of the site, David Robinson, identified a number of areas and buildings on the South Hill that could have been used for public activities, and he named the area the 'Civic Centre' (1930: 16–28). In the northern section of the South Hill he found two long buildings whose shape suggested a non-domestic function, but he could not clearly ascertain the use of the buildings. Robinson suggested that they could have been a barracks, a *stoa* or an arsenal (1946: 309–12). The area to the south of these contained a large building, which Robinson believed to be a *prytaneion*—a civic building—with rooms for dining and for civil, military and religious officials. The building measured 32m x 16m and contained four *apothekes* or storage pits cut inside the building and twenty-two outside. Robinson suggested that the *apothekes* stored food, for dinners in the *prytaneion*, yet the material evidence here is not entirely consistent with his identification of the building's use. At the end of the *prytaneion* was a portico that was set aside for bathing, with pieces of terracotta bathtub or basin; this is a practice without parallel in any other classical *prytaneion*. There was monumental masonry in the form of large ashlar blocks among the remains here that dated to the fifth century BC, yet, curiously, the building did not exist for as long as the settlement survived; its south end was built over by houses. In light of this uncertainty, the term Civic Centre seems a rather optimistic description of the area. It is possible that the building on the South Hill fell into disuse when the new settlement was constructed and that new administrative buildings were set up on the North Hill.

In the southern portion of the North Hill, Robinson found another area that may have had a public use (1946: 79–82). Again, though, the material evidence is not conclusive. The section contained an open area, which Cahill suggests was an agora (2002: 32), but it bears no resemblance to the Athenian Agora, being simply an open area and about a quarter of the size; there are no material remains that clearly indicate what activities went on here. While it may have provided an area for markets, the open area could have equally been used as a gathering place or, as the excavators Robinson and Graham suggest, for military manoeuvres (1938: 21–2). As a result of political instability in the region, the Olynthian cavalry and army often engaged in warfare, and this would have provided an ideal place to muster the troops (Xenophon *Hellenica* 5.3).

The open area has three buildings placed around it that may have served non-domestic roles. Across the northern limit of the open area lies a rectangular building that has a similar shape to a *stoa*. With dimensions of *c*.75m x 9.5m, it is not a large building— the South Stoa in Athens measured *c*.100m in length—and it has no monumental architecture and no activity-related finds. To the east of the *stoa*-type construction is a building that the excavators suggested was a *bouleuterion*, a council chamber linked to the organization and administration of a city. There is little evidence here of monumental architecture; it contained a single preserved column drum *c*.1.30m high and two complete Doric capitals, both covered with fine white stucco. A row of seven columns on limestone bases ran down the centre of the building and there were some palmette antefixes in the vicinity but these were not exceptional or monumental and similar antefixes were also present in the private buildings A v 7 and A v 10. There was a dressed stone foundation and a higher section at the west end, which may have been for seats. The '*bouleuterion*' contained 218 coins and some weights—items that Cahill suggests are more easily associated with commercial behaviour than administration (2002: 265). It could have operated as a meeting place for magistrates, as did the South Stoa at Athens, but the idea that the building was part of a 'public' zone is diminished by the fact that the '*bouleuterion*' did not face onto the 'agora' area but opened onto Avenue B. The last 'public' building identified at the site was a fountain house, adjoining the '*bouleuterion*'. The fountain house was rectangular in shape with a tiled floor and water basin in its south-west corner. Water was supplied by underground aqueduct, through terracotta pipes in a tunnel three metres below the surface. The water came from the Polygyros Hills, eight miles away. The provision of water and the construction of buildings suggest that there was a degree of centralized management within the community, but the indeterminate nature of the spaces and the absence of monumentalization imply that the community did not view or use its urban space in the same way as classical Athens.

While it is hard to identify public buildings at Olynthus, it is impossible to find evidence for public religion. Robinson identified an area on the South Hill as a religious zone due to the discovery of a double row of stones from the pre-Persian period at the site, which might have been part of a long rectangular altar (Robinson 1930: 16–28). Unfortunately, the stones could not be linked to any building, use or users; it is impossible to say what they are or why they are there with any degree of certainty. On the east side of the hill Robinson found fifty terracotta heads, some from the early sixth century BC, including *protomes*. These masks are often found in temples and Robinson felt that the deposit pointed to the existence of a temple or a shrine in the locality. However, closer investigation by the excavation team revealed that the terracotta figurines were present in a building that appeared to be a house. There were no temples or shrines on the North Hill and, although an inscription was found outside the city referring to 'the sanctuary of Artemis at Olynthus', no contender for this place has been located (Cahill 2002: 32). The excavators also searched for the theatre that they believed had existed in a large sloping semi-circle of land at the side of the settlement but no evidence of theatrical performances or citizen gatherings was ever found here.

We thus have no clear evidence of 'public' behaviour in Olynthus. There are no buildings that can clearly be linked to the administration of the city, there is no temple or evidence for other religious buildings and artefacts used by the community as a whole. Neither is there any clear sign of commercial behaviour in the area identified as an agora. Most evidence at Olynthus comes from the private buildings at the site—in fact, the whole of the new area constructed in the 'synoikism' appears to be a residential district. There are large houses in the Villa Section and on the East Spur Hill. Long, rectangular houses are placed against the city walls and smaller houses with dimensions of approximately $17m^2$ are constructed in a grid pattern on the main body of the North Hill. These buildings in the grid system contain a mix of residence and production or industry, similar to what we have already seen in Athens. There is evidence for the production of sling-bullets, terracotta figurines and textiles, as well as the processing of agricultural products, and these activities seem to be spread through the houses at the site. The material evidence from Olynthus differs significantly from the Athenian pattern. Although industrial activities are integrated into residential areas at both sites, Athens is dominated by remains from the 'public' sphere, with its administrative and religious buildings standing out clearly within the urban landscape; at Olynthus public buildings are conspicuous by their absence and it is the house that dominates our view.

The houses at Halieis

At Halieis we have evidence of public and religious buildings (Ault 2005). The most prominent public building project was the large strong wall that surrounded the city. The wall had towers overlooking the gates and the land beyond; it was not simply a monumental statement: it acted as protection for the inhabitants as their city was a pawn in the power games of larger neighbours. Within the city walls was an acropolis. Although this has a shrine area and the remains of an altar, it was not an exclusively religious area, as the Athenian Acropolis was. The acropolis at Halieis also contains the remains of barracks buildings, indicating that it was a defended or defensive site. Similar barracks buildings can be found next to the city walls, a testament to the uncertainty of life at Halieis. There is little evidence of other temples or monumental religious buildings in the city, but a small shrine room was set into the city wall and a number of small street shrines have been located among the private buildings at the site. These are dotted throughout the city, so that there is no clear evidence for a single religious zone in Halieis.

Areas associated with public activities or administration have not been identified within the walls at Halieis. No agora has been located and no evidence of monumental public buildings has been found. While this might be the result of the piecemeal nature of the excavation, we must also bear in mind that it may indicate a different conception or use of urban space. The only building of a public nature is a building in the eastern half of the city, which has been identified as a mint. Lying below the acropolis was an area named the 'Industrial Terrace' by the excavators (Jameson 1969). In one of the buildings here were large storage vessels or *pithoi*, a ceramic basin and a rectangular depression with two small square holes. This may have been a dye-works or an area for extracting oil from olives on a large scale. The archaeology of this area is confused and difficult to read and there are also indications of habitation in the buildings here. The layout of Halieis and the architecture of the buildings do not indicate that public activities were located in specific zones in the city.

The organization of Halieis bears similarities to both Athens and Olynthus. As in Athens, industrial activities took place alongside residential activities. In both Olynthus and Halieis, religious and public activities are not as clearly visible as those of Athens. Halieis is also similar to Olynthus in that its houses are clearly visible. Excavations in the lower portion of the town uncovered a grid arrangement that was similar to the layout at Olynthus (Ault 2005), but the buildings set into the grids were irregular in size and quite small. Where Halieis differs significantly from our two previous sites is in its management of interior and exterior urban space. Beyond the city wall there is evidence of large-scale building projects and monumental construction. There was a harbour, which connected to the Argolic Gulf, a temple of Apollo was situated to the north-east of the Hermione Gate and an extra-urban sanctuary of Demeter to the south of the city. There was also a monumental building called the Hypostyle Hall whose use is unclear but whose layout suggests a public function. Again, we have a very different representation of the relationship between public and private space in a classical Greek city. Once more we have unique elements that show another attitude to the role of the house in Halieis.

Observations

The three sites are very diverse. At Athens there is a distinct focus on the public sphere—private spaces and houses are irrelevant and invisible. At Olynthus we have the opposite: a massive residential sector with little evidence of public, religious or economic buildings or zones. At Halieis, we appear to have evidence for the concentration of activities in certain areas but this is structured via the use of space inside or outside the city walls.

What can we learn from the differences between these sites? Before we begin to examine the links between urban structure and urban ideologies, we must acknowledge the possibility that the variations between the sites may have a pragmatic basis: they may be a consequence of settlement size, settlement type and the survival of sources. The area inside the walls of classical Athens was approximately 225 hectares. To put this into perspective, the medieval walls of London enclosed an area of 134 hectares. At Olynthus, the overall area of the site is around 90 hectares, which might be compared with the area inside the medieval walls of St Albans, England, which was 81 hectares, making Olynthus a large town, or small city. In contrast, the area inside the walls at Halieis was only 18 hectares, even smaller than the Roman military fort at Caerleon in Wales, whose area was 20.5 hectares. It is understandable that larger settlements would have more space and greater access to resources; they also have a greater ability to construct monumental buildings. Thus in Athens we can clearly separate monumental public and religious structures from other buildings in the city. At Olynthus, the smaller size of the site creates a closer relationship between public and private activities in order to accommodate the needs of household and community in a smaller area. Hence we see a mixing of activities and a blurring of the boundaries between them. At Halieis, where the area inside the walls was severely limited, public and religious buildings may have been constructed outside the walls simply as a result of spatial constraints.

There are also differences in the quality and availability of evidence at the sites. Athenian builders used stone to create their monumental buildings. It is possible that in smaller, less wealthy settlements the inhabitants used cheaper materials that did not survive. Public buildings may have been equally important in all three sites but our view is dominated by Athens, due to the durability of the building materials. The poorer quality of private buildings at Athens makes them harder to uncover and 'read'. Centuries of rebuilding at the site have also reduced the possibility of understanding fully the relationships between public and non-public areas. At Olynthus, the effects of abandonment, erosion and ploughing have also undermined our ability to read the evidence clearly, but the absence of any rebuilding has left us with a sizeable sample of plans and remains. The reason for the dominance of the house in the material record at Olynthus may reflect its history. The site was a 'new' city and the absence of public buildings may indicate that we are looking at a proto-urban development. Had Olynthus endured, it is possible that monumental buildings would have been constructed; the dominance of houses may reflect the priority of sheltering the new community. The excavation at Halieis was inhibited by its piecemeal nature because work could only take place as plots of land became available to purchase (Ault 2005: 1–11). We do not yet have a full picture of ancient Halieis, and the areas outside the city may exert a more dominant influence on our view of spatial organization here.

Although these are valid reasons for differences in the archaeology of our sites, the variations may also reflect different political ideologies. The Athenian democratic constitution placed an emphasis on the people as a political body—hence the importance of public and religious buildings and the degree of visibility afforded to them through monumental construction and decoration. Private spaces and houses should not be so apparent because that would detract from the democratic ethos. The absence of large public sites and the mixing of public and private spaces at Olynthus could be indicative of a different type of political organization. Olynthus was formed by the *synoikism* of many communities. Its use of private buildings for political and religious needs may reflect the importance of keeping many groups happy and preventing any single group from dominating. The evidence may point to an oligarchic rather than democratic constitution that meant that law courts and political meeting places capable of holding the citizen body were not necessary. The absence of temples could also reflect that Olynthus was part of an *ethnos*, a community comprising a number of urban centres that all used a central site with religious and political buildings. This central site may have been the place where monumental display was considered acceptable rather than in the urban centres. Halieis was constantly fought over by larger, more powerful cities. Its emphasis on defence and protecting its people and their houses may be a natural consequence of this.

The way that communities construct and manipulate urban space can tell us much about urban society. A contextual study of the built environment in classical cities allows us to identify differences in the organization of sites and to examine the various ways that communities created and managed their lives. When we look at the house as a functioning part of the urban landscape rather than as an isolated and separated enclave, we can truly begin to consider the role that the house and its users played in the political social and religious life of its community.

At Athens, Olynthus and Halieis there are significant differences in the presentation and arrangement of houses within the urban landscape, as well as differences in the structure of urban space. This undermines the use of Athenian texts to create a model for urban and domestic space and reinforces the conclusion that the house played a different ideological and practical role in each of our cities.

CHAPTER 2

HOUSE AS HOME
VIEWING THE CLASSICAL GREEK HOUSE

As we have already noted, houses are not just a means of providing shelter; the house itself is an ideological construction that encodes the beliefs and practices of the group that uses it. If we analyse the floor plans of houses in 'new' cities and in more modern housing developments from the USA and UK, we can see connections between the organization of domestic space and beliefs about public and private life. The house is private; a visitor must enter through the single main door at the front of the house. This often leads into a transitory zone such as a hall, where the visitor is inside the house and yet has restricted visibility and access to other rooms. Spaces that it is acceptable to enter are placed in close proximity to the hall, such as living rooms or dining rooms. Spaces that are exclusive to the family are made less accessible: the bedrooms are often placed upstairs, the kitchen and bathroom associated with the intimate activities of eating and washing are at the rear of the house. A second entrance may lead into a private yard or garden. Rooms are named according to the activities that take place in them and they contain a set of artefacts and features that relate directly to those activities. In studying modern western houses, we gain a dual perspective; we can see what activities take place in the house and how they are managed. We can consider what defines a house and can create a model for the 'ideal' house based on the location, appearance and internal arrangements of the buildings that we find. Bearing this in mind, we will now turn to look at our ancient cities. We will seek to identify houses and to consider what 'house' meant to the communities at Athens, Olynthus and Halieis.

Athenian texts

We begin our quest to identify Athenian houses by considering the information that texts can offer us about the appearance of residential buildings. Although houses appear in classical Athenian texts on many occasions, detailed descriptions of the physical presentation of houses do not. Xenophon and Aristotle discuss the house in two philosophical works, both called *Oeconomicus*. Both texts are concerned with household management and discuss issues such as the relative position of the house: 'I showed her that the whole house fronts south so that it was obvious that it was sunny in winter and shady in summer' (Xenophon *Oeconomicus* 9.2–4). Aristotle agrees with this, adding only that the house should be longer than it is deep (Aristotle *Oeconomicus* 1345A–B). Both authors discuss the ideal house, using ideas about the house and its management as a metaphor for the organization of society and state. As a result, the information that they reveal about the house is tantalizingly incomplete. Xenophon notes the importance of having specific rooms for certain activities, such as the storage of food, as well as separate rooms for male and female slaves to sleep (Xenophon *Oeconomicus* 9.2–5). Yet we are not told where these rooms can be found in a house, or how they appeared. The few details that the passages do offer tell us little. Houses have rooms and doors, they have some decoration and they may have outbuildings. The references to outbuildings and the descriptions of working land in the books by Xenophon and Aristotle suggest that they are not writing about townhouses but the management of country estates. Indeed the advice to make the house long and broad conjures up an image of the Vari House, set in isolated countryside and with no restrictions on its size, shape and relative position. The 'ideal' house is not really a suitable model for urban residences.

References to urban housing in classical texts tend to be more fragmentary as the appearance of the house is usually incidental to the narrative rather than its central topic. Texts indicate that there were many types of houses in Athens, differing greatly in the quality of material used in their construction. Some of the houses were poor, with toilets outside the front door and walls so thin that the residents could dig through them (Aristophanes *Women at the Thesmophoria* 484–5; Menander *Phasma* 49–56). The regulations that Aristotle describes, to prevent upper storeys and buildings projecting over the streets, suggest that houses could be small and cramped (Aristotle *Oeconomicus* 1347A; *Constitution of Athens* 50.2). The poor state of urban housing is mentioned explicitly by Isocrates when he contrasts city and rural houses (7.52). Demosthenes also refers to the quality of urban housing in his comparison of rich contemporary houses with the more simple houses of the past (3.25–6, 13.29, 23.207). Some houses were modest: the house of Euphiletos has two storeys, a bedroom, a room with a couch and hearth, an inside water supply and an exterior door to the street (Lysias 1). Some citizens clearly live in large luxurious houses. The house of Callias has a *peristyle* court and sufficient rooms to host a large philosophical 'sleep-over' (Plato *Protagoras*). In a legal speech by Demosthenes, the speaker mentions his smallholding near the Hippodrome (47.53–7). The plot has a house with a garden and a tower room where the female slaves live. The houses that appear in law court speeches and the houses of philosophical tracts tend to be used by the writers for ideological purposes. Despite probably being based on reality, it is difficult to know which parts we should accept and which reject; so these longer descriptions cannot be relied on to provide us with a clear model for the urban house.

Other passages offer smaller snippets of information and, although many are isolated and fragmentary pieces of information, there is some consistency in the descriptions from which we can learn basic information about the appearance of houses in Athens. We know that houses might be of more than one storey, as plays refer to the use of stairs within houses (Aristophanes *Clouds* 1485–8; *Women at the Thesmophoria* 481–3; Menander *Samia* 20–1). We know that urban houses had flat roofs—it would be rather difficult to host the Adonia festival on a slanting roof (Plato *Phaedrus* 276B; Aristophanes *Acharnians* 262). We know that houses frequently opened onto the main street (Aristophanes *Women at the Thesmophoria* 481–3) with a staggered entry system of *prothyron* doors that prevented passers-by from looking in (Aristophanes *Wasps* 802). We know that the houses had courtyards (Aristophanes *Wasps* 1215; Demosthenes: 47.53–7), and that separate places were created for men and women within the house (Demosthenes 47.53–7). Again, the fragments offer insights but not knowledge; we do not have enough consistent information to construct a general model for the appearance and organization of the Athenian house using texts alone.

Using material evidence

While our texts offer oblique insights, archaeology has the potential to give us a clear view of ancient houses. Surprisingly, though, the question of how to identify houses remains relatively unconsidered in discussions of classical archaeology; few scholars deal with the fundamental issue of how we can or should identify a classical house. As a result, houses tend to be identified by a process of elimination: they are buildings that are not in a public area, have no monumental decoration and are not large in size. In his article on domestic space in the Greek city-state, Michael Jameson sought to expand on this basic approach and to establish more clearly the characteristic features of the classical Greek house (1990: 97–8). Using a combination of data from a detailed reading of textual sources and observations from urban excavations, Jameson set out the key features of the classical house. He noted that in its external aspect, the house was a closed unit with a restricted entrance, a few narrow windows and an invisible interior. The internal spaces of the house consisted of a central courtyard, around which the rooms were arranged and occasionally with a stair base, indicating an upper storey. Jameson linked the shape of the house to the gender ideology expressed in classical texts: high walls and small windows indicated a desire to keep internal spaces private; restrictions on access and the presence of a central courtyard allowed the movement of women within and in entering and exiting the house to be observed and controlled. In our investigation of the material evidence, we will follow Jameson's basic model and look for small buildings with central courts, rooms placed around the court and a single entrance to the street. Other architectural or spatial features that we might use to supplement this model and distinguish a residence from another building include the presence of private or separated groups of rooms within the internal spaces of the house and evidence of embellishment. Households can separate their spaces and restrict access to them to differentiate private family areas from rooms that are open to guests and will often personalize their spaces with decoration. Although not all of these features may be present in a building, they offer us a starting point for our quest to identify and investigate classical Athenian houses.

Viewing the houses of classical Athens

Jameson's study suggested that the courtyard, located in a central position, was an essential feature in any classical house. Buildings with a central courtyard and surrounding rooms certainly can be found in Athens, such as House C in the Street of the Marble Workers and the Central House excavated on the north-east slopes of the Areopagus that consisted of ten rooms around a central courtyard (see **Plan 1**, p. 173, and **Plan 2**, p. 174). Yet there are many buildings where this canonical layout is not followed. In the House of Mikion and Menon—an incomplete house located in the south-west corner of the Agora—the small irregular court was situated next to the street and surrounded on only three sides by approximately ten irregular rooms. In the Flugelhofhäuser found on the Pnyx Hill the buildings were divided into two wings, placed either side of a rectangular court. The four houses in a block located on the north slopes of the Areopagus have no uniform plan to their internal divisions. The north-east house has a central court, with rooms opening off it, whereas the south-east house has its court in the south-east corner. House M18, next to this block and House O18 to the south of the Agora consisted only of two covered rooms. They had no courtyards. There is a high degree of variation in the presence and location of a court in Athenian private buildings; we can only say that the existence of a central court, while persuasive, does not necessarily prove that a building is a house, or that the absence of a court means that it was not a house.

Another important feature in Jameson's model is the presence of a single street entrance. If we look more closely at the layout of the buildings identified as houses in Athens, we can see that not all of them follow this pattern. Indeed, many of the buildings have single rooms or units of rooms in the same building with separate entrances onto the street. In House C on the Street of the Marble Workers, Room 12 opened directly onto the street while Rooms 10 and 11 were joined to form a unit separated from the main building by a wall, but still utilized the main access route to the street. The rooms on the west side of the Areopagus housing block had many different street entrances. It is possible that the different entrances imply that there were separate living quarters within a single building; they are not evidence of a house but of houses, areas inhabited by different social or familial groups. In some cases, the divided spaces have evidence that is not obviously domestic in nature. The buildings in the Street of the Marble Workers contained indications of trades such as marble working and the dyeing of textiles. A three-room unit in the block of buildings at the foot of the Areopagus ended in a space with evidence of food preparation, while another unit had a room at the back with storage *pithoi* sunk into the floor. Young suggests that Room 12 in House C was a shop (1951: 207). The divisions and different entrances indicate that the buildings are not exclusively domestic but are multi-use buildings with part used for residence and part for non-domestic activities, whether commercial or industrial.

Rooms within the Athenian buildings are often organized into discrete suites with a single entrance onto the courtyard.

This means that the rear spaces in the suite can only be reached through internal rooms—access is controlled and visibility is restricted. The West House on the north-east slopes of the Areopagus had a series of rooms towards the rear that could only be accessed through internal spaces (see **Plan 1**, p. 173). House C had a restricted room to the north-east of the court (see **Plan 2**, p. 174). We tend to interpret these units as private family space, yet this notion is based on the belief that the whole building is the setting of one family. This is a cultural expectation based on life in contemporary western houses. If we put aside the assumption that these buildings are a single house, it is possible to speculate that, far from controlling access, the courtyard enables access to the groups that reside in the building. In modern Iranian houses the courtyard is a communal space rather than a controlling space; it is an access and open area for all the residents inhabiting the building. The divisions in space may reflect the presence of different groups of residents. One courtyard building may house a number of different unrelated groups, and the units around the court may indicate divisions between these groups. There may be many 'houses' within a single building.

Evidence of decoration in Athenian private buildings is notable by its absence. In the vast majority of the buildings identified as houses there is no evidence of paint or decoration and the floors are of beaten earth or clay. This is the case in fifth-century BC buildings, such as the House of Simon, the House of Mikion and Menon and houses in the Street of the Marble Workers. Some plaster was found on the walls of Houses C and D but there is no trace of paint and the plaster may have been set up to ensure that the wall was waterproof. It is only when one moves away from the Agora and from houses of the fifth century BC to houses of the fourth century BC that some evidence of decoration in the form of floor mosaics can be found. Even this decorative evidence is not sufficient to identify the buildings as domestic; the mosaics may point to another, non-domestic, use of space. A large building in the Kerameikos area had signs of decoration in rooms (O and P), as well as a simple mosaic pavement that linked the two areas of the house (Knigge 1991). This building is often described as a brothel rather than a house, with the mosaics indicating that the rooms were decorated to make them attractive to customers. The building at 9 Menander Street consisted of two adjoining rooms with pebble mosaic floors (Graham 1966). The floor of the outer room had a large mosaic of concentric circles and geometric designs. An off-centre doorway led into another room, which had a raised platform along the walls and a mosaic floor in the centre. These were the only two rooms found, and their size and lack of a connection to other spaces may indicate that we are looking at a discrete unit that was not designed for domestic use. Its dimensions and elaborate decoration again suggest a desire to create an attractive space and to draw in customers.

A connection between the decorated mosaics and commercial practices can also be seen in the Central House on the north-east slopes of the Areopagus, which had three rooms with some form of mosaic flooring (see **Plan 1**, p. 173): on the west side there was a suite of two interconnected rooms with a mosaic floor in the outer room; to the south of the main door was a room with a raised cement platform around the walls and a central mosaic of dolphins and sea monsters; to the north of the main door was a room with a plain mosaic floor of white marble chips. A cistern containing large quantities of pottery relating to eating and drinking was found outside the room with the dolphin mosaic. The quantity of pottery suggests that the building was used for large-scale drinking or dining—the spaces have a commercial rather than a domestic function. When mosaics are found in contemporary excavations, the evidence is often fragmentary, and whole buildings are not usually recovered, so we cannot know with certainty how the space was used. We can only say that the presence of a mosaic floor is not proof that a private building is a house.

Decisions about whether or not an Athenian building is a house are difficult, as we appear to have no way of providing a universal definition. We must look at the architecture and decoration of each building in context—one definition does not fit all buildings in Athens. In the crowded city where space was at a premium, larger buildings served a number of purposes, whether residential, commercial or industrial. Evidence further suggests that small buildings without any of the features set out by Jameson, such as M18, could act as homes. Although we can identify private buildings in Athens, it is not as easy to identify and explore houses.

Domestic ideology in classical Athens

So far our investigation has taken a material perspective in seeking physical evidence of houses, using texts to assist in the process of physical identification. Yet, as we have already noted, houses also exist in an ideological sense. If we return to the texts and search for information about attitudes to the house rather than material descriptions, this can also teach us something about the classical Athenian house.

The first interesting fact to emerge from a re-examination of the texts is that Athenians had no clear word for 'house'. Where people live is an *oikos*, which can mean all the possessions of a household, including slaves, as well as the buildings that they live in, or it might be a *stegos* or *melathron*, meaning a roofed space, or a *domos*—a built place. There is no obvious rationale that governs which particular word is used. Thus, the word *domos* can refer to a temple (Aeschylus *Eumenides* 205) but as *domation* can refer both to the whole house (Aeschylus *Agamemnon* 968) as well as to a single room in it (Lysias 1.17, 24). An *oikos* can be a palace (Aeschylus *Agamemnon* 867), a tent (Sophocles *Ajax* 65) or a temple (Herodotus 8.143). It can be a whole place of residence (Theophrastus *Characters* 16.4) or just a room within it (Xenophon *Symposium* 2.18). Even within a single play, different words can be used to describe the same residential building. In Euripides' *The Madness of Hercules*, the paternal home of Hercules is referred to as a *domos* (138–9), an *oikos* (327–31) and a *melathron* (336–8). The terminology in classical texts simply indicates a differentiation between the natural and the built environment. 'Houses' appear not to have existed in a modern linguistic sense.

So, if texts use generic words, how does the audience or reader identify that a building is a house from a description alone? When a character uses the word *domos* how do we know whether he is talking about the place where he lives or where he keeps his animals? If we look more closely at texts, we can see that the meaning of 'house' or 'home' is given to a building by linking it to the father or paternal ancestors (Aeschylus *Agamemnon* 518). This connection between father and building is given added impact by including the hearth in the reference. Ajax on returning home exclaims: 'O sacred soil of my homeland, O Salamis, O seat of my paternal hearth' (Sophocles *Ajax* 859–60). The links to father and hearth are not just a feature of tragic poems. In the forensic speech 'Against Demosthenes', the prosecutor asks how the jury could afterwards bear '... to look upon your father's hearths' if they acquitted an individual (Dinarchus 1.66). The same idea of shameful behaviour, contradicting the importance and central role of the family in Athenian life, is implicit in Lycurgus' assertion that an individual betrayed his father's hearth

(Lycurgus *Against Leocrates* 131.5.7). The symbolic connection of family and hearth lies at the root of Herodotus' reference to the hearths present in a community as a means of indicating how many households lived there (1.176). Only a member of the family has access to family celebrations traditionally associated with the hearth, children of the family share the same father figure as its head, so the father or paternal ancestors and hearth become a way of adding meaning to a building and defining it as a family home.

This way of defining and identifying private space gives it a flexibility that modern domestic space does not always have. The houses in our modern new cities were built specifically for residence. They have a particular appearance and certain common features such as bathrooms, which are placed with a degree of permanence as a result of the need to connect pipes and sewage facilities. The private buildings of Athens appear to be blank canvases, capable of changing their role according to the needs of the occupants. This means that a building can change from being a domestic space into being a workspace or even a religious space in a short period of time. This perception of private space is reinforced in a passage by Aeschines:

> For it is not the dwelling places nor the buildings which give their names to those living in them, but it is the inhabitants who give to the places the names of their own practices . . . And if by chance a doctor moves into one of the workrooms on a street, it is called a practice. But if he moves out and a blacksmith moves into the same workroom, it is called a smithy . . . (Aeschines 1.123–4)

A house is not a discrete building with a single exclusive use—it is a building being used at that moment for the purposes of residence. A house is identified by the people who live there and by the activities that they perform in the building. Hence there is no specific word for 'house' and houses do not require description in texts. The behaviour of their occupants reveals their use.

The passage by Aeschines offers us a further insight into the concept of 'house' in classical Athens. It is only the 'workrooms on the street' that have the meaning of 'smithy' and so on. The rest of the building in which the rooms are located may have a different meaning. This enhances the impression given by our study of material evidence: a house does not have to be a whole building but can be a portion of it. The pattern of land ownership in Athens meant that only a citizen could own land and property. Yet while a property had to be owned by a citizen, it could be used by anyone. The city of Athens was large and contained non-Athenian Greeks, slave households and foreigners with *metic* status. These people and their families required somewhere to stay either permanently or when visiting the city for business reasons. Athens had a thriving leasehold market, and legal speeches indicate that different users could lease portions of the same private buildings (Osborne 1988). So, Philoneus rents a room in Athens while Philondas leases property there as a *metic* (Antiphon 1.14; Demosthenes 49.26). In these examples, the arrangement is described by the use of the word *synoikia*, which means 'living together'. An owner might thus maximize his revenue by hiring his private building to different groups of users. Isaeus mentions an Athenian *synoikia* in the Kerameikos where Euctemon installed his mistress Alce as manager and went himself to collect the rent (Isaeus 6.21). The Old Oligarch notes that the people of Athens profit from trials of allies held in the city as they make money from leasing *synoikia* to them (Pseudo-Xenophon 1.17). In the speech 'Against Stephanus I', a husband leaves his wife a *synoikia* in his will, so that she can acquire income (Demosthenes 45.28). Pasion is described as lending money on the security of land and *synoikia* (Demosthenes 36.6). The evidence suggests that buildings rented out to more than one individual or group and owned by another were not an unusual feature of city life. The place where people lived—their house—did not have to be a whole building but could be simply a few rooms in a larger building.

The classical Athenian house, as presented in texts, is essentially a built environment. Its meaning is given by its users and use and this has the potential to change as the occupants alter. So, private buildings could vary between residential, commercial or even religious uses. As the users changed, the meaning of the space changed. A house could also consist of a single building or just a few rooms in a larger building, existing alongside evidence for commercial or even industrial practices. It is the people and their needs that give the spaces their meaning.

Olynthian houses: the evidence of inscriptions

Although we have no texts from Olynthus, we have a number of leases and house sales relating to the buildings, which could help us to identify and examine houses here. The word *oikos* is used to refer to a building, as in Athenian texts, and buildings are identified more specifically by reference to owners or residents of adjoining properties, such as, '. . . the *oikos* next to the *oikos* of Demarchus' (Robinson 1934: No. 4). However, we cannot be sure that *oikos* indicates a house. The Demarchus inscription was found in Building A v 10, Room (g), and further notes that the sale of the property is to include 'the room with the *pithos* and all the income-producing things'. A *pithos* is a large storage vessel and its appearance in this way suggests that the building had a place for storage. Similarly, a loan inscription between

Lycophron and Hegias and Anthes reveals that the property on which the loan is based shall exclude 'the room with seven couches' (Robinson 1934: No. 6). The two inscriptions reveal that rooms in buildings could be owned or disposed of separately. The room with the *pithos* could have been left out of the sale but it is included. It might have been retained by its original owner or sold to a third party. It was seen as separate from the building and required specific inclusion in the contract of sale. Similarly the seven-couch room is specifically excluded from the lease—it is separated from the remainder of the building. It may have been kept in the control of the lessor or may have been leased to another. We cannot be certain of the exact motive for separating these rooms from others in the building but can be sure that rooms in the Olynthian buildings were capable of being owned and used by different people. They were not exclusively domestic in use nor the discrete setting for a single family, as modern houses from the USA and the UK tend to be. At Olynthus, we appear to have a pattern of domestic spatial use that is similar to Athens, where buildings could potentially host a number of different uses and different types of users.

The style of the inscriptions also offers us an insight into the idea of space at Olynthus that further undermines the possibility that the buildings are exclusively domestic. Spaces in these buildings are not identified by names that indicate a definitive or permanent link between the space and the activities of the family that uses them. There are no 'bedrooms' or 'living rooms'. The 'room with the *pithos*' in the Demarchus inscription may indicate a space used for storage; some of the buildings in Olynthus had rooms with *pithoi* present, either scattered around or actually embedded in the floors, as in the Villa of Good Fortune. However, the phrase does not mean that this room would always be a storage space; it might simply have been used for this purpose at the moment of the sale. Unfortunately we have no idea exactly what the income-producing things were. This could refer to the sale of slaves, resident in the building, who make a particular product and so bring in an income, or to Room (g) itself, which brings in income from hire. The linguistic style shares a pattern with the loan inscription between Lycophron and Hegias and Anthes and its exclusion of 'the room with seven couches'. As we will see, there are a number of rooms with cement borders in the houses of Olynthus that have been identified as male dining rooms. Yet it is not the perceived function of the space that identifies it but the artefacts that are present within it. Buildings at Olynthus appear to be regarded as capable of supporting different users and different uses; spaces in Olynthian buildings are identified with a terminology that hints at a flexible and changeable use of space.

Viewing the houses at Olynthus

We will turn now to look at the buildings and consider the question of whether we can identify houses in the material remains at Olynthus. The excavators at Olynthus, Robinson and Graham, were certain that the buildings at the site were residential (1938). They created a plan of the model Olynthian house, which is a discrete building with a central court, single entrance and private groups of internal rooms. How far is this accurate? The buildings of Olynthus are not uniform but take a range of different shapes. The buildings on the South Hill, the oldest part of the settlement, show little consistency in their size or presentation. The buildings on the North Hill can be separated into groups: there are large, long buildings in Row A, against the west wall of the city, square buildings with sides of approximately 17m in the grid section at the centre of the North

Hill, buildings with more inconsistent shapes on the East Spur Hill and larger buildings outside the city wall, to the east of the city in the Villa Section. Despite these differences, the internal arrangements of the Olynthian buildings have many similarities. Most of the rooms in the buildings on the North Hill and in the Villa Section are articulated around a courtyard and porch area, or *pastas*, usually placed in the north of the house (see **Plan 4**, p. 175). The method of entry into the building varies, with either a 'staggered' entry through a *prothyron* or room, or entry into the court or porch area. The larger rooms tend to be placed in the north of the building between the porch area and the north outer wall. The southern rooms flank the court or are positioned below the court adjoining the south wall, and are generally smaller than the north rooms. The arrangements of the buildings in the Villa Section and Row A also tend to follow the general rule of placing a porch area to the north of the court with larger rooms to the north of the porch. The buildings on the South Hill, by contrast, have a highly irregular arrangement of rooms. There is no sign of a clear court or porch area and often it is difficult to see how the rooms relate to each other. The reason for this irregularity is antiquity: the buildings on the South Hill are part of the original settlement at Olynthus while those on the North Hill and in the Villa Section are more regular as a result of the speed of their construction. These newer constructions are part of the *synoikism*, the joining of disparate communities to create a new settlement, mentioned by Thucydides (1.58–9).

The descriptions above reveal general patterns, yet closer study of the buildings on the North Hill shows that there are a number of significant variations to these models. The courtyard moves its position and takes different shapes. In A viii 3 and A viii 5, the courtyards are on the west side of the house, rather than being central. In A vi 1 the courtyard is in the south of the building while in A vi 10, it is not surrounded by rooms but has one room to the south and two to the north. The courtyard in A vi 10 is simple, consisting only of beaten earth. This contrasts with A xi 9, where the courtyard has a *peristyle* and takes up two-thirds of the available space in the building, the remainder of which consists of only three small rooms to the north of the *peristyle* court. Although the width of the buildings in the North Hill grid is regular, the overall size of the buildings can be different—some are larger or smaller than the average size of 17m². Within the grid blocks that usually accommodate ten buildings are some larger edifices that take up the space of two buildings. In Block A viii, buildings 7 and 9 have been joined to make a single structure. This appears to have been achieved by the simple process of knocking down the wall between them. In Block A v, a large building takes the space of Building A v 6 as well as half of the neighbouring A v 8, which is reduced considerably in size as a result. But, rather than being a simple expansion, Building A v 6 appears to have been conceived of as single building. It has a central courtyard with a setting for an altar and a *peristyle* court and the rooms are ranged around the north, east and west sides of the building. Building A v 8 is thus a very small building next to A v 6, with two rooms in the south, one of which contained the door to the street, and two rooms in the northern part. The courtyard area in A v 8 is large by comparison with the rooms, taking up roughly 42 per cent of the internal area of the house.

The houses of a modern urban housing development, such as the Thornhill Estate in Cardiff, Wales, all have an identical pattern in the organization of space so that the buildings differ only in size. The inconsistency in the buildings in the Olynthus North Hill grid supports the idea that, although they were built at the same time, the buildings were shaped for different uses and by different users. Some buildings clearly subdivide into separate quarters, often with their own entrances to the street. Buildings A vii 9 and A iv 9 are divided into two units (see **Plan 3**, p. 174). The outer unit adjoins Avenue B and consists of three discrete spaces with openings into the avenue; the inner section has an entrance to the street from its northern side. A similar arrangement of space can be found in B vi 9, where the rooms opening onto on Avenue B could be shops or small spaces rented for temporary or guest residents. Our study of Athenian texts indicated that one room could be a perfectly adequate residence for an individual whose main residence is elsewhere and only occasionally needs to enter another town (Antiphon 1.14). There is no reason why this could not be equally true in Olynthus—all cities have visitors. In B vi 7 a cross-wall separates a unit of three rooms (a, d and f) from the rest of the building; in A viii 10 the division is equal, resulting in two separate buildings on a single plot; in other cases a single room is separated from the rest. A vi 8, A vii 3, A vii 8, A viii 6 have large areas set aside that run the length of the building. In A v 10 and A vii 9, a single, long room is separated from the main building with its own entrance onto the street. Robinson and Graham suggest that these rooms are stables (1938: 210–11).

The proportion of decorated spaces is higher in Olynthian than Athenian buildings. Some of the buildings had mosaic floors; some had painted walls, yet we cannot assume that the decorated spaces are domestic. Robinson and Graham report that of the sixty-five complete houses excavated by 1938, at least thirty-two had one or more rooms decorated with painted stucco walls (1938: 291). The most common type of decoration consists of blocks of colour applied in a single, dual or tripartite system of bands, and appears to focus on one or two rooms in the buildings. While it is possible that this indicates residential use, it is also possible that the decoration indicates a more public use of the space. Although all of the buildings were identified as houses, buildings such the Villa of Good Fortune with its decorated mosaic floors, central altar and porch surrounding the court on all four sides have an air of monumentality that is more akin to public buildings. Similarly, the room decorated with a mosaic of Bellerophon in Building A vi 3 lies directly opposite an altar, giving a line of vision from the place of sacrifice to the place of dining (see **Fig. 4**). This seems more compatible with the spatial arrangement of a temple than a house.

The layout of the Olynthian houses supports the impression given by inscriptions that buildings are not exclusively residential. Their spaces are separable and capable of being owned or used by a number of individuals. Any decision to see these buildings as entirely residential or as the location of a single family means

4 *Bellerophon mosaic from Building A vi 3, Olynthus*
(photo J.E. Morgan)

that we ignore evidence for the divisibility of internal spaces and the potential for numerous owners and occupiers in one building, not all of whom may have been using the space for domestic purposes.

Viewing the houses at Halieis

The number of houses completely excavated from Halieis is small: five houses with fifty-seven rooms (Ault 2005). The houses come from different sections of a city grid system (for plans of the buildings, see **Plans 7–10**, pp. 176–8). House 7 is situated in Area 7 by the south-east gate. It lies at the southwest corner of a block of approximately ten buildings. The remaining buildings are situated nearby in Area 6. House A lies in the northeast section, close to a public building, the Mint. It is on the southwest corner of a block. The three remaining houses, C, D and E, are situated in the same row, with D and E adjoining in its southern half and C in the north. House 7 and House A have been excavated more fully: House C, House D and House E have large areas that could not be excavated.

There are many similarities in the design and spatial organization among the houses of Halieis. The largest space is the courtyard, which is most frequently placed in the south-west corner. This is true even where the building is on the north side of a row, as is the case in House C. Rooms are positioned to the north of the court and occasionally to the east of it. Entry to the buildings is either through a *prothyron* or porch entrance into the court or, in the case of House C, through a room in the north of the building. There are suites of rooms in the buildings, which may suggest that they were used by a number of different social groups. House 7 is separated into three clear groups of rooms; Rooms (7-9) and (7-10) form one suite while (7-11/12/14) and

(7-16/17) are the other two. In each case the groups of rooms have separate entrances to the court and do not interconnect. This is a pattern similar to the Athenian and Olynthian buildings. In House A, we can again see groups of rooms but these do not open onto the court. The rooms are all situated to the north of the court. Room (6-83/84) can only be accessed via Corridor (6-86) while Rooms (6-87/88) are next to them and accessed via the porch area. Although this arrangement does not discount the possibility that the spaces were used by different groups, it is a different layout to those we have encountered at Athens and Olynthus. House C presents another very different layout. Entry is into area (6-63), onto which Rooms (6-60), (6-61) and (6-64) open. None of these rooms is connected. In the south-west corner of Room (6-63) a small corridor leads into a courtyard with two suites of rooms, (6-64/65/66) and (6-57/58). Neither suite is connected. This arrangement with suites of rooms opening off a court might be more in line with Athenian and Olynthian buildings but the access route, through a room and corridor is certainly unusual. With House D and House E, it is by no means certain that we are dealing with two discrete buildings. Not only do we have separated suites of rooms, but the room groupings have separate entrances to the street, rather than opening off a court. In House D, Rooms (6-26), (6-27), (6-28) and (6-29) form a discrete unit with a separate entrance from the street. In House E, Rooms (6-21) and (6-22) are a unit of two rooms with access from the street, while Rooms (6-11) to (6-13) also appear to be separate and entered from an alleyway opening off the street.

The buildings of Halieis are not decorated as lavishly as their counterparts at Olynthus. There are no decorated mosaics in the houses, and floors are usually beaten earth—with a few exceptions where they were either paved with cement or with plaster but not painted. There is very little evidence for colour and in most cases where plaster is on the wall and floor of a room, it is for utilitarian purposes. Only one Room (7-9) has a cement border at its edges. This room also had evidence of red plaster on the walls and floors. Coloured wall plaster is also present in House 7 (7-10), House A (6-87), House C (6-54), (6-55) and House D (6-28). House 7 (7-12) has a white circle marked in pebbles on its floor but the reason for this—whether decorative or functional—is unclear.

Observations

When assessing the buildings of a classical city, we identify houses because they are clearly not public buildings and can be fitted into the spatial pattern of domesticity that we expect to see. Athenian texts have traditionally provided the basic model for these patterns of domestic behaviour. The house is seen as being a single discrete building, the location of a single family group. Yet the investigation of texts here suggests that if meaning is added by users and use, a house is simply any place where people live. This flexibility appears to be reflected in the material remains. Instead of a single entrance, many of the buildings have multiple entrances, indicating that different groups could use the spaces within them. Instead of always having a central court, the layout of houses at each site differs: some houses have a central court, some have none. Not all of the buildings have decoration and, where we do find it, we still cannot connect it clearly to domestic behaviour. One model does not fit all.

The buildings at each site show interesting differences in their organization and layout. At Athens and Olynthus the courtyard position may alter, but it always offers a central access point for the rooms and suites of rooms grouped around it. In these cases it is easier to see the building as the locus of many 'houses' rather than the place of a single family group. The differences in arrangement may be related to the nature of the settlement. At Athens, the constantly expanding population meant that spaces for habitation were in high demand, and an Athenian citizen could make money by dividing properties and leasing their separate parts. The need to provide accommodation quickly may also explain spatial arrangements at Olynthus. Here the properties were divided into tenement-style accommodation in order to provide a place for the incoming refugees and their businesses. At Halieis, the buildings identified as houses have the court placed in the south-west corner rather than the centre of the building. Rooms are most frequently grouped together to the north of the court and access to the rooms is usually through other, internal spaces. The city of Halieis is small and, although this does not preclude the possibility of multi-functional buildings, the fact that the buildings have single street entrances and the manner in which the internal spaces are grouped and linked suggests that they are being used by a single group.

In studying the classical Greek house, investigators tend to explore without defining the subject of their investigation. They presume that buildings are houses; they presume that the buildings have a single role and purpose—that of domesticity. If we put aside the assumption that these buildings are houses, we are able to build a more nuanced understanding. If we overcome our cultural expectations of the domestic context and view buildings as private rather than domestic, we can more fully appreciate the range of roles, including social or residential, that the buildings performed in their specific community.

CHAPTER 3

THE FAMILY AT HOME

In modern western thought, the house is intimately connected to the family. It is the place set aside for them within the city, it is the stage on which the private dramas of family life are played out. This link between house and family is embedded in the modern psyche to such an extent that it underscores the terminology we use to describe houses. Their rooms are kitchens, bathrooms, living rooms and bedrooms; we transcribe the activities and needs of the modern family onto the spaces where they live. Unfortunately, we also use this language to define and describe the spaces in classical houses. This modern, culturally based, terminology dominates our view of the ancient architecture and allows no room for different interpretations. Yet our studies so far have shown that the buildings identified as houses in classical cities were not used exclusively for domestic purposes and that constant references to buildings as 'houses' obscures our view of the way that domestic life was organized within the classical city. It is time to change the direction of our investigation. If the house is the place of the family then, rather than searching for architecture, it may be more productive to search for users. Can we locate the family? What can we learn from this about classical houses and classical society at Athens, Olynthus and Halieis?

Identifying the Athenian family

We begin our investigation with a study of Athenian texts. Who was in the Athenian family and what was family life? Texts offer us many different views of family arrangements. Evidence from philosophical tracts appears to indicate that the classical Athenian idea of the family fits with the modern conception of the nuclear family. Aristotle notes that the essential building blocks of a household are the master and slave, husband and wife and father and children (*Politics* 1253B). In *Laws* Plato suggests that married couples should leave their old homes and parents behind and start a new household (776A–B). Yet the nuclear family is not just an ideal created by philosophers. In the speech 'Against Marcartatus', Demosthenes describes how Buselus divided his property between his five sons, each of whom took a wife and had children, so that five new households came out of his original one (Demosthenes 43.19). This picture of a house containing mother, father, children and household slaves is also a feature of tragic and comic plays. Despite their affairs, Agamemnon and Clytemnestra form a basic family unit with the children, Iphigenia, Orestes and Electra (Aeschylus *Agamemnon*). Admetus lives with his wife and children (Euripides *Alcestis*). Dicaeopolis lives with his wife, daughter and slaves (Aristophanes *Acharnians*), as do Philocleon (Aristophanes *Wasps*) and Myrrhine (Aristophanes *Lysistrata*).

There are also many examples of households that do not fit with this model idea, and texts that indicate a different picture of domestic arrangements. We should not be surprised by the range of people that live together and the unusual family arrangements created by this—emotional and familial complexity is not the sole preserve of modern life. In his speech 'Against Eubulides'

Demosthenes offers a view of how re-marriage could alter the landscape of the family. The mother married Protomachus and had two children; she then married again and had the defendant (Demosthenes 57.40–1). As a result, many of our pictures of mother, father and children mask the more complicated reality that one of the parents is a stepmother or stepfather to the child. In *Hippolytus* the eponymous son lives with his father, Theseus, and his stepmother Phaedra (Euripides *Hippolytus*). Electra lives with her mother Clytemnestra and her second husband Aegisthus (Aeschylus *Libation Bearers*). Apollodorus was brought up by his mother and her new husband, his stepfather Archaedamus (Isaeus 7.7). The wife of Phormio brought up her son from a previous marriage with her new husband (Demosthenes 36.8).

As a result of remarriages and death, we often find references to older children living with only one parent or living with a parent in the family home after marriage. In *Clouds*, Strepsiades lives with his son and slaves (Aristophanes *Clouds* 1–24), and in *Peace*, Trygaeus lives with his daughters (Aristophanes *Peace* 110–23). Theodote lives with her mother and looks after her financially (Xenophon *Memorabilia* 3.11.4); Evergus lives with his father (Demosthenes 47.35). In Aristophanes' *Women at the Thesmophoria*, a widow describes having to make money to support her family (445–58). After marriage Euphiletos moves his wife into the house where he lives with his mother (Lysias 1.6-7). There are also many cases where the guardianship of children and sometimes their mother has passed to the most senior male in the family. If the mother is alive, it is sometimes difficult to tell from the text whether the adult male with guardian responsibility actually lives with the family. In the court case 'On the Property of Aristophanes', the father-in-law is described as the guardian but there is no indication that he lives with the mother and children (Lysias 19.8–9). In 'Against

Diogeiton', the guardian clearly does not live with them, as the widowed mother and her children live alone in the Piraeus and the guardian appears to have his own family (Lysias 32.7–8, 17). In contrast, when the guardian in 'On the Estate of Cleonymus' dies, the new guardian, their grandfather, takes the orphaned children to live in his house (Isaeus 1.12).

One occasion when the guardian does live in the same house as his charges is when he has taken responsibility for orphaned women who are of or near marriageable age. In this case the women are vulnerable and need to be controlled in order to protect their reputations and the legitimacy of their children. It is the job of such a guardian to give the women away in marriage. So, Aristarchos is left caring for fourteen sisters, nieces and cousins after revolution leaves him as the male head of the household (Xenophon *Memorabilia* 2.7.2–12). The speech 'Against Simon' records the horror of the speaker when Simon burst into the presence of his sister and nieces, violating his protection of them (Lysias 3.29). Ties of blood bind these groups but there are instances when these ties are stretched and residential groups created out of more disparate individuals. If a man had no sons to pass his land and property to, he could adopt an heir who lived with him: Apollodorus was so grateful to his stepfather that he sought to adopt his stepfather's grandson Thrasyllus (Isaeus 7.14–17). Similarly Menecles was allowed to adopt a son, and the maternal grandfather Xenaenetus adopted Cyronides when he had no sons of his own (Isaeus 2.13–18, 10.8). In other cases, acts of the guardian or head of the household created more unusual families. So Pericles, as the guardian of Cleinias, took him away from his brother and placed him in Ariphon's family to be educated (Plato *Protagoras* 320A); Orestes was sent away from his own home to be fostered (Aeschylus *Agamemnon* 879–81); Agamemnon intended to bring Cassandra into his house as his concubine, to live alongside his wife and children (Aeschylus *Agamemnon* 950–5); and Chrysis is a concubine living with her master in Menander's *Samia* (21–8). The affairs of Callias also created a complicated scenario whereby he lived with his wife and her mother, the latter of whom became pregnant by him (Andocides *On the Mysteries* 1.124–9).

It is also possible that individuals from outside the immediate family could share the family house or building. In 'Against Evergus' an elderly freed slave who had looked after the speaker as a child returned to live with the family (Demosthenes 47.55–6). The son, in the speech 'On the Prosecution of the Stepmother for Poisoning' describes how there was an upper room in their building that was occupied by a friend, Philoneos (Antiphon 1.14); we cannot tell if this room was hired out from within the speaker's house or was simply another room in the same building that was not owned by the speaker or Philoneus— either possibility is feasible. Texts show us that a range of people of different genders, age groups and social groups could live together as a family. The composition of the family is fluid and adaptable; its members are created by personal circumstances and personal choices.

Family life at Athens

We turn now to the issue of family life and, in particular, to the question of what acts we can specifically link to the life of the family. The main purpose of a house is to shelter the family group; it provides cover and permits social interaction. As a result, texts indicate that the main activities performed by families at home relate to the basic needs of sleeping, eating and drinking. Xenophon observes that one should take lunch in the house but avoid getting too full (Xenophon *Oeconomicus* 11.18).

He also paints a picture of domestic harmony at Thebes where Leontiades reclines on a couch after dinner while his wife does woolwork (Xenophon *Hellenica* 5.4.7). In 'Against Evergus', the two accused burst into the house and find the mother dining with the children in the court (Demosthenes 47.53). A fragmentary passage from Menander's play *The Door Keeper*, included in Athenaeus' *Deipnosophistae* (71E–F), describes a family drinking together at home on a formal occasion. In *Wasps*, references to smoke evacuation suggest that a space was set aside in the house for food preparation (Aristophanes *Wasps* 135–41).

Textual examples of individuals sleeping in the house are harder to come by, as it is an activity of little interest to the reader or audience. In *Clouds* Strepsides and his son are sleeping in the same room (Aristophanes *Clouds* 1–24); there is no mention of furniture or beds and Strepsiades only describes his son as sleeping deep in his blankets. In the law court case 'On the Murder of Eratosthenes', Euphiletos describes how, having been locked in a room by his wife, he went to sleep (Lysias 1.12–13), but unfortunately we are given no idea of the appearance of the room and whether he lay in blankets or a bed. We know only that it was an upstairs room but this could have been the result of the rearrangement of his house after his baby was born.

The family cannot survive without constantly replacing the members that it loses and so it is no surprise that texts show the house is a hub of sexual activity. This sexual activity is both marital and extra-marital. In comedy, Lysistrata refers to wives putting on see-through gowns, presumably in the hope of attracting their husband's attention (Aristophanes *Lysistrata* 42–5). In *Wasps* the father brings a girl home from a party for sex, while a reference in *Peace* to the joy of finding a serving girl inebriated has a clear implication (Aristophanes *Wasps* 1368–79; *Peace* 535–7). There are also references in forensic oratory. In 'On the Murder of Eratosthenes' the wife makes a joking reference to her husband having sex with the slave girl if she leaves the room (Lysias 1.12); later in the same speech we find that she is the one committing adultery: she brings a man into the house for sex and is caught naked with him by her husband and his friends (Lysias 1.14, 20, 24–5). Direct references to sexual activity are surprisingly uncommon in texts: sex may have been viewed as an intensely private activity and not a suitable subject for literature or, as seems more likely, the sex lives of others was of little interest to the audience, except as a comic scenario or scandalous tale.

The natural result of sexual activity is children, and the house provided a place of shelter for the next generation. Despite the vital importance of children to the family, children and their behaviour in the house rarely provide the subject matter of texts, where they appear only when their behaviour impinges upon the lives of adults. There is a baby in 'On the Murder of Eratosthenes'—we are only told that it cries and requires milk and water (Lysias 1.9–12). Agamemnon's daughter Iphigenia sings for guests in her father's dining room (Aeschylus *Agamemnon* 243–5), while a young boy, Autolycus, joins his father at a male dinner (Xenophon *Symposium* 1.8). There are references in texts to children playing and to the toys they played with: in *Clouds*, Strepsides boasts of the toys that his son made for himself when young (Aristophanes *Clouds* 877–81). These included houses and boats of clay, leather chariots and carved animals, and Xenophon mentions the dolls played with by children (Xenophon *Symposium* 4.55). Plato recommended that children should develop skills for their future working lives through playing with miniature versions of the tools they will use or actions they will perform (Plato *Laws* 643B–C). Unfortunately, most of the descriptions we have of games come from much later sources, but it is reasonable to assume that toys were used by the children of a family even though we lack descriptions of the games played with them.

A family is constituted as much by their behaviour and participation in shared rituals as by their blood relationship. As such, basic needs become woven into more complex behaviour that reflects and reinforces family ties. The house is a locus of food preparation, and many of these occasions are part of the ritual fabric of family life. Acts such as cooking and consumption become most visible in our texts when the house is to celebrate or entertain guests on the occasion of a rite of passage. In *Samia* the women of the house are described as bustling around preparing food for a wedding ceremony (Menander *Samia* 206–50)—many of the plays by Menander end with a wedding and thus focus on the preparation of food and altars and the decoration of the house for the ceremony. Similarly, at the end of *Peace* the house prepares for the wedding of Trygaeus (Aristophanes *Peace* 1316–59), while in the speech 'On the Estate of Chiron' a wedding feast is mentioned as evidence of legitimacy, citizenship and inheritance (Isaeus 8.18.5–6). Other family occasions such as the Tenth Day Feast after birth and the *perideipnon* after the funeral also take place in the house (Demosthenes 40.29, 40.59, 18.288; Menander *Aspis* 222–33). The consumption of food and drink in the house also becomes visible in textual sources on occasions when the residents of the house entertain non-family members. In tragedy, Hercules is entertained in the palace of Admetus, and the palace of Agamemnon has guest quarters set aside for unaccompanied male guests (Euripides *Alcestis* 544; Aeschylus *Libation Bearers* 712). In Plato's *Symposium* an entertainer is sent from the male party to the gathering of women in the house (176E). Sometimes guests are entertained in the house, but there is no mention of food or drink, only conversation, although these occasions tend to be the discussions of philosophers (Plato *Republic*; Plato *Protagoras*).

Texts also describe domestic ritual occasions, where the family prepares and consumes food as a part of cult rites. Cephalus sacrifices in the court of his house at Piraeus (Plato *Republic* 328C), and in 'On the Estate of Chiron', the speaker describes an occasion where he and his family performed rites in honour of Zeus Ktesios while they were in his grandfather's house (Isaeus 8.15). In *Acharnians* Dicaeopolis cooks the food for a cult celebration and creates a cult procession (Aristophanes *Acharnians* 887–8). Both Agamemnon and Hercules participate in family sacrifices at the altar in their house (Aeschylus *Agamemnon* 1035–8; Euripides *Hercules* 922–30), and the women of the household celebrate the festival of the Adonia on the roof of their house (Menander *Samia* 38–46). These occasions will be discussed in more detail in Chapter 6, but at this stage it is important to observe that texts show ritual eating and drinking to be a natural feature of family life within their house.

The archaeology of the family

If the place of the family is a home, then texts indicate a host of people and activities that we could reasonably expect to be associated with a house. What can a study of material evidence add to our understanding of families and the family home? First, although we would have difficulty in identifying family relationships through material evidence alone, archaeology may be able to help us to ascertain the ages and gender of people using a particular ancient building. Certain artefacts may be more likely to be used specifically by men or by women. Athenian texts link some items, such as loom weights and cooking utensils, to female domestic activities, and the presence of these items could indicate that adult females lived in the house. Similarly, the presence of agricultural tools or fishing hooks might suggest a male presence. Unfortunately we have no way of assessing the social status of the individual user—weaving, fishing and cooking were just as likely to be activities performed by slaves. The resident might thus be a male citizen with slaves to perform his domestic chores, but we cannot tell this from the material evidence. We can only tell that the building or part of a building was used for residential purposes. Personal artefacts such as jewellery, a stylus for writing and male toilet items such as a *strigil* or scraper can all show that private activities were performed in the space. We may also see evidence that children resided with the adults through the presence of personal items such as a baby's feeder bottle or children's toys and games.

Secondly, archaeology can also provide evidence of domestic behaviour in the residues of acts that relate to private activities. Our study of texts showed that the six principal acts relating to the domestic environment are cooking, eating, drinking, washing, sleeping and sexual intercourse. However, there are difficulties in trying to identify the material remains of these acts and using them as evidence of family behaviour. Our first problem concerns the availability of evidence. The act of sexual intercourse is unlikely to leave remains that we can identify and so can be excluded from our search. A second difficulty is that we cannot always tell how the artefacts were utilized by the user. Evidence for the act of washing—either the individual or the individual's clothes—may be shown by the presence of specialized equipment such as *louters* or washbasins and baths, but a bowl and sponge could equally have sufficed. A *louter* may also have been used to grind corn or mix dough (Cahill 2002: 168–89). Similarly, the acts of cooking, eating and drinking can all occur at public establishments. The principal difference between private and public residues in respect of these actions might be only a matter of scale: the quantities cooked will be greater and the floral and faunal remains of meals will be more extensive. Commercial or public establishments will therefore require a greater number of cups, plates and bowls (Kelly-Blazeby 2007), but plain cooking pottery is under-reported in excavations, which makes it difficult to establish if commercial or domestic food preparation was taking place. Finally, we must retain an awareness of context. For example, Building MN has a washing area and an area for eating and cooking; although it is a small building, this would not necessarily preclude its use as a residence. It is, however, in the sanctuary of Demeter and Kore at Corinth (Bookidis 1993). If we looked at this building without taking into account its context, we might see it as domestic—evidence must be considered fully in its unique context before we reach any conclusions.

Houses are canvases for family life; where we find evidence of residential behaviour, we can explore the possibility that we have found a family and their house. However, we must maintain a degree of caution. We cannot use artefacts conclusively to assign individuals or activities to specific spaces: it is possible that the presence of the artefacts reflects a place of storage rather than a place of use. In seeking to assess whether a building or area of a building is residential, it is better to take a cumulative approach. A single room with a feeder bottle tells us little. A unit of rooms within a private building where we have plain pottery, evidence of cooking and eating, a bath and a range of private artefacts associated with men, women and children is more likely to indicate a residential presence. Finding families in material remains is not an easy exercise.

Families in classical Athens: the material evidence

We shall turn now to look at private buildings in classical Athens. Finding evidence of different ages, genders and private activities is extremely difficult in the buildings here. Although items were found on house floors, these were not generally published because excavators were more interested in red-figure vases and cared little for coarse pottery or small figurines. The Athenian buildings are currently being reinvestigated by Barbara Tsakirgis, and more detailed evidence will be published in due course. Unfortunately, even with complete publication, the amount that we can learn from artefacts within the houses is limited. The fill in Room 5 of House C had a *pyxis* and a *lebes gamikos*—artefacts associated with women (Young 1951; see **Plan 2**, p. 174). These might indicate the presence of women but cannot tell us with any precision which parts of the building the women used or whether they were free women or slaves. The constant need for urban space in Athens meant that buildings were cleared and re-built many times over. The vast majority of domestic artefacts are therefore in wells where they were dumped after these clearances and it is not possible to tell which items belonged to which buildings, let alone to which part of the building. The Athenian family left no material trace in the houses of classical Athens. We have little choice in our investigation but to rely on architecture and texts. Texts show that residence took place but architecture offers us no clue of where the residence occurred or how the use of space in the buildings was organized.

Families in Olynthus: the material evidence

In contrast to the private buildings at Athens, excavation of the buildings at Olynthus was relatively thorough and well reported.

Although we are not always given details of the quantity and quality of plain pottery in a building, we are at least told of its presence. As a result we can look more closely at the types of activity that were carried out within the buildings. Given the degree of potential for variation in the remains and artefacts present in the buildings, a general study of the whole site would not do justice to the evidence. We will therefore focus specifically on the material from four buildings that best illustrate the problems and benefits of trying to identify family activity and houses in the classical buildings of Olynthus.

Building A iv 9

This building is situated on the north-east corner of Block A iv on the North Hill (see **Plan 3**, p. 174). It is to the north of the area called the agora and is a 'model' house in size and shape, being 17m², which is the average size, but the house is unusual for a number of reasons. First, the space is clearly divided into two areas, one with an external aspect and the other with internal spaces. The external area consists of three rooms adjacent to Avenue B and with entrances onto it. There is no communication within these rooms or between these rooms and the main portion of the building. Over ninety coins were found spread through these rooms, and very few artefacts were present, suggesting that the rooms may have had a commercial purpose. The remainder of the spaces were internal, accessed only through a single door onto Street V, which led into Room (c). While the single door can be seen as indicating a need for privacy and evocative of domestic needs, this possibility is diminished by the fact that the front door opens into a room, rather than a court or porch as is usually the case in Olynthian buildings. Room (c), the entrance chamber, has an area of central ashes, showing that a fire was made there, and the room also has a hollow base near the north-west corner, a portable altar, a marble basin pedestal and pottery. A pendant and earring were also present. Adjacent to Room (c) was Room (b), a rectangular space connected to (c) via a partial wall, constructed with a pillar partition. These areas are identified by the excavators as 'flue' spaces, created for the extraction of smoke. Room (b) contained a pendant, a female terracotta figurine, a plaque with an image of a woman and a bull, and a fishhook. The jewellery suggests that there was a female presence in the house, and the nature of the evidence implies that this was connected to domestic activities. It is however, difficult to see this area as a space used by women due to the proximity to the street, which contradicts ideas about female seclusion within classical Greek society, an issue that we will explore in more detail in Chapter 5.

The building has a second unusual feature in the presence of another combination of two rooms, (j) and (k), that are similar in structure to (b) and (c) and appear to have served the same function. Room (k) (the flue) was smaller in size than Room (b). It was paved with flagstones and had a heavy deposit of ashes, indicating that cooking had taken place here. Room (k) was joined to Room (j) by a smaller pillar partition. The two rooms contained a miniature drinking cup, a *pyxis* and lid, a figurine of Hermes, cups, plates, a jug, a fishhook and a terracotta plaque showing a man and a horse. Between the two groups of rooms lay a very small court, Room (h), and a long porch area, Room (e). At the western end of the porch were two rooms, (a) and (g), facing each other. These two rooms and the space of the porch between them yielded a number of interesting artefacts. Items in Room (a) included thirty-one loom weights, a mould of a seated boy and a terracotta medallion with a picture of Athena on it. In the porch were a grain mill, a terracotta basin pedestal and pottery connected with pouring and drinking. In Room (g) were eighty-three loom weights, another terracotta basin pedestal (*louter*), a grain mill, a miniature cup, two mirrors, keyhole reinforcers and a fishhook. This area thus has evidence for weaving work but also for food preparation and possibly washing, as well as personal items with strong female connections such as mirrors and jewellery.

There is no clear evidence in the building of commercial or economic activities—the archaeological evidence appears to be purely domestic. So, is this a house? The arrangement of the material indicates that the building could have contained two families. The duplication of spaces might reflect that each had their own areas marked out within the same building; the single entrance may even be a sign that the two groups were related. Although we can clearly see artefacts that indicate a residential presence in the building, we cannot see the social status of the occupants—we do not know if they were slaves or freemen. It is possible that the presence of two cooking areas is related to a need to divide domestic space between free residents and their slaves. The evidence from A iv 9 indicates that buildings in the North Hill grid could be divided internally to create different residential spaces and that these could have been used by social groups who perceived themselves as separated, whether by blood or social status. The evidence for domestic activities and the presence of personal items strongly suggest that the dominant role of this building was residential.

The Villa of Good Fortune

The evidence from A iv 9 contrasts with the evidence from the Villa of Good Fortune (see **Plan 4**, p. 175). Both properties were excavated at the same time, so we cannot argue that later excavations were more efficient: there were simply fewer artefacts to find in the villa. The villa is unusual for the number and detail of mosaics that it contained: in Room (a) was a mosaic of Dionysus and the Maenads, and in the attached anteroom Room (g) was a scene of Thetis giving armour to Achilles. The shape of this suite of rooms implies that they were used for dining but we have no clear evidence to suggest the gender of the diners or the nature of the occasions that took place here. While the term 'villa' suggests the residence of a wealthy family, the lack of finds and elaborate decoration in the house may indicate that it was a commercial building with rooms available for hire. This possibility is strengthened by a study of the second suite of decorated rooms. Room (e) had a mosaic with a wheel pattern and inscription, while the mosaic in inner Room (f) had a central square and inscription around it. The inscriptions read ΑΓΑΘΗ ΤΥΞΗ – 'Good Fortune', ΕΥΤΥΞΙΑ ΚΑΛΗ – 'Good Luck is Beautiful' and ΑΦΗΡΟΔΙΤΗ ΚΑΛΗ – 'Love [or Aphrodite] is Beautiful'. Robinson suggested that these were good luck mottos, just as a modern householder might have 'Bless this House' at the front door. However, the names have cultic links and it is interesting that the central square of the mosaic in Room (f) was of sufficient size to hold a small, portable altar. Again, the rooms contained few artefacts—only one female head and a number of coins were present. There is nothing to connect the spaces clearly to domestic activities.

The villa had a number of entrances. To the north and south, two external doors led into corridors that gave access to the court. The court itself was a *peristyle* court with covered porches on all four sides and a large altar base at its centre. The size of the court indicates that it could have been used by large groups of people. The porch areas contained very few artefacts. The exception was Porch (k), which had eight relief vases in the shape of heads. These appear to have fallen from a shelf along which they were placed. A third entrance led from a side street into Room (j). This room had four large terracotta jars, fixed into the floor for storage. The other rooms in the house were equally bare. Rooms (b) and (c) in the north of the villa were identical in form to Rooms (b) and (c) in A iv 9, yet had no finds apart from some coins and no evidence of fire. The large-scale storage, the evidence of elaborate rooms for dining or socializing and the presence of coins scattered through them hints that the ground-floor spaces were used for commercial purposes. The presence of a stair base suggests that the building had an upper storey, and this may have housed a family group, but there is no way to investigate this and we can only conclude that the villa was not a house.

Building B vi 7

Building B vi 7 has a single entrance onto the street, which comes into a small corridor (see **Plan 5**, p. 175). The internal areas are divided into three separate zones. The first zone opens to the west off the entry corridor and is a unit consisting of three areas, Room (a), Room (f) and Porch (d). The second zone is situated at the end of the entry corridor in the south of the building, while the third zone consists of Porch (e), a covered area opening to the east of the entry corridor and Room (c), which is accessed via this space. There are interesting differences in the artefacts present in each of these three sections (Robinson 1946). In the east suite, Room (a) had an altar, a terracotta *protome* figurine (a shape linked to sanctuaries) and a terracotta head of the god Attis; in Room (d) there were some jugs and cups, a vessel for containing liquid and a large pot; Room (f) had a cement border and was painted red. It contained some large plain vases, a red-figure *pyxis* and a large statue of Asclepius made of marble—one of only two marble statues found at Olynthus. There is no evidence of cooking fires in this suite and, although, there is evidence of eating and drinking here, the area appears to have been used for cult rather than family life.

The arrangements of space in the eastern unit are difficult to assess with clarity. Although two rooms, (c) and (e) were identified, the area has a number of small cross-walls that may indicate further internal divisions here, and the artefacts offer little insight into the use of the rooms. In Room (c) there was a bronze bead, an *oinochoe* or jug, a figurine of a dancing girl, fragments of other figurines, a *krater* and several loom weights. Room (e) had red plaster on its north and west walls. There is not sufficient evidence in these spaces to see them as residential. The decoration, spatial separation and lack of artefacts may indicate a reception area or even a commercial area of a poorer quality than those in the Villa of Good Fortune.

In contrast to the east and west suites, the southern rooms contained a great deal of residential evidence. The stone-paved court, Room (g), had fragments of plain pottery for eating, drinking, pouring and storage. Further items for preparing and serving food were found in Room (j), together with personal items such as a fishhook, a paste bead and a small lead statue of male and female herms. The court also contained the remains of part of a bathtub. The type and range of pottery found with evidence of domestic behaviour and personal items could suggest that this area was used for residential purposes while the remaining units in the building were not.

The spatial arrangement of B vi 7 offers a number of possible interpretations. First, we could see the divisions as signs of separate use and users, with a cult area and commercial area existing alongside a domestic space. There is no reason why a family could not live in intimate proximity to a shrine. The 'house' appears to be only a portion of the building here. Secondly, the presence of the single main entrance may indicate that, although spaces were divided into different activity zones, they were owned or used by a single group. The west suite might have been a family shrine and the east area their domestic reception rooms. Yet the size of the cult suite—taking up approximately a quarter of the space in the building—seems excessive. In combination with the reception rooms to the east, this may indicate that the shrine was owned or cared for by a resident family but available for general use. The presence of a marble statue of Asclepius, altars and bordered space for couches could imply that the suite was a shrine sacred to the god and used by a resident priest for healing rites. The building is therefore not a house because its spaces are not exclusively residential, but it is possible to argue that the building contained a house. Building B vi 7 offers us a fascinating insight into religious behaviour at Olynthus: religious space and domestic space co-exist comfortably in the same structure. We shall return to the issue of religion again in Chapter 6.

The House of Many Colours

Our final building contains evidence of work, the provision of services, commerce and also residence (see **Plan 6**, p. 176). The courtyard, Room (i) contained the base of an extremely large altar, which faced the entrance to the street. The possibility that certain spaces in this house were used for religious purposes is strengthened by the evidence from a unit of rooms, (g), (h) and (k), behind the altar. Room (k) contained a square hearth with grey ash, three storage amphorae and fragments of two female figurines. The small room (g), which was attached to Room (k), had some lamps, a jug and a female figurine. It also had a bathtub. There is little in the artefacts found in these two rooms to suggest that they were residential. This is confirmed by Room (h), which was attached to Room (k) by a pillar partition. Room (h) contained a large trench, in which were found bones from cows, sheep, goats, pigs and deer; the flesh of the animals had been prepared and cooked at this spot. Also present in the room was a rich assemblage of artefacts, including twelve terracotta figurines and twenty vases, mostly used in the serving of food and drink. It is easy to see a connection between these two rooms with sacrifice taking place at the altar and the flesh being cooked in Room (h).

In the north-east of the building the complex of two rooms, (f) and (d), offered a place at which the meat could be consumed. Room (d) was a formal dining room with coloured paint on the walls and floors. Room (f), which was also decorated, offered exclusive access to Room (d) and contained bosses from a storage chest as well as plates, a *krater* fragment and a bead. It is not clear where the door to Room (f) lay—it may have opened into the porch area Room (e) or into the entrance area adjoining the court and next to the main door. While we cannot say which is correct, the latter possibility would allow us to reconstruct the south side of the house as a space separated for religious or commercial reasons, with an area for sacrifice and cooking and an area for dining. The remaining room on the south side of the house is Room (m). This room contained four large *pithoi*. As with Room (j) in the Villa of Good Fortune, this suggests that the area was used for the storage and possibly the sale of a particular product or supply of food to customers in the building.

The northern part of the house contains a unit of rooms with a strongly residential flavour. The porch area, Room (e), held two small altars and a marble *louter*, as well as a range of pottery for eating and drinking. Room (a), in the north-west corner of the building, contained fragmentary pottery with traces of paint and painting equipment as well as forty-one loom weights, a spindle whorl and an *epinetron*, used in wool working. There were also miniature cups and many items for eating, drinking, serving and pouring. Room (b), which was attached to Room (a) by a pillar partition, held thirty-four loom weights and pottery connected with drinking, as well as some figurines. Personal items in the form of tweezers and a fishhook were also present in the two rooms. Room (c) contained only fragments of hardware and coins. There is a dearth of plain pottery in these rooms but the range of pottery, personal items and the contrast between this part of the house and the remainder suggest that these rooms served residential purposes.

We do not know what was taken from these buildings; we can only see what was left. Our study of these four buildings shows that there are many difficulties in finding families and in identifying houses at Olynthus. Although residence can clearly be observed in some portions, it cannot be in others. Equally, some buildings have no evidence for residence at all. We can only work with the remains that we have and, at Olynthus, these support the idea that spaces in the buildings were often used by different social groups and for different purposes—one of which was residence.

Families in Halieis: the material evidence

As at Olynthus, the buildings of Halieis contained a range of artefacts and features with the potential to be read as residential evidence (Ault 2005).

House 7

House 7 (see **Plan 7**, p. 176) contained a great deal of pottery with connections to every stage of cooking, eating and drinking. The number of vessels estimated to have been found in the whole building was at least 824, 60 per cent of which were in the area of the court. This figure includes pottery found in the pit feature (*kopron*), which would appear to indicate that the area contained items discarded when the building was abandoned, or just before. However, as the majority of storage vessels were found within the court, the discarded items may be masking a possible role of the court as a storage space. The remaining artefacts were spread through the building, with two interesting assemblages in Room (7-12) and Room (7-16/17). Room (7-12) contained a concentration of fine-ware vessels for drinking and serving. In his study of the buildings, Ault suggests that (7-12) was a living area and formed part of a suite with a bathroom (7-11) and secondary space (7-14) (Ault 2005). This is an interesting idea that seems to be based on the size of the rooms and room functions in suites from Olynthus. Room (7-12) contained no other evidence with residential potential: items found here included a *pithos* lid fragment, a stone button, a circular mould and possibly the metal end of a staff. Room (7-14) held only a chisel and, although Room (7-11) is the smallest in the house, there is no evidence that it is a bathroom. There is no bath and the walls and floor are not plastered. Neither is there any residue from domestic actions such as cooking, eating or washing.

The second concentration of artefacts is in Room (7-16/17). This room contained a large hearth with evidence of fire *in situ*. The connected rooms contained twenty-four cooking vessels, forty-six vessels associated with serving and consuming food and twenty-seven pieces of fine-ware pottery. These certainly appear to support the identification of the area around the hearth as a kitchen. The area also contained a few personal items, consisting of a *pyxis* lid, a spearhead fragment and a possible mirror handle. There is evidence of cooking, but this is not necessarily domestic. A large concentration of pottery associated with eating and drinking was found in a deposit just outside the house, and Kelly-Blazeby (2007) suggests that the amount of pottery in the house was too great for domestic purposes. She argues that Rooms (7-9/7-10), a dining room and antechamber, were commercial premises. This is a very persuasive argument and indicates that, like Olynthus and Athens, the buildings at Halieis could host a number of different functions. But can we see this as evidence of different users in the same building? The spatial arrangements of House 7 are not easy to read. There is one entrance from the street, a *prothyron* entrance, which leads into the courtyard. Once inside, there are few restrictions on access as all the rooms open onto the court or porch area with only two exceptions (7-11 and 7-14). It is possible that this was a building used as a home and also as a commercial premises by a single family group.

House A

Our second building at Halieis is House A (see **Plan 8**, p. 177). This comprises three units of rooms and holds a wider range of artefacts that can be seen as residential. The unit at the rear of the house, Corridor (6-86) leads to Rooms (6-83) and (6-84), which may have had some industrial or commercial purpose, as shown by the size of the cement platform and the plaster on the walls. In Room (6-83) beyond the plaster platform were two miniature shapes, a mirror fragment, an amphora, some cups and a bronze distaff. There were fifteen cooking vessels in the room and the walls were decorated with red and yellow plaster. The small room (6-84) had plaster on its walls and floor, suggesting that it was used for a wet activity, such as washing. In Corridor (6-86) were the rim of a *louter*, a miniature dish, a red-figure jug and a fragment of a grinding slab. The function of the unit cannot be ascertained from its architecture or artefacts, but the personal nature of the items present, the decoration and the presence of a washing vessel is persuasive evidence that women worked or lived in the building here.

To the east of this unit lie two interconnected rooms, Rooms (6-87) and (6-88). Room (6-88) had a cobbled pavement and interior well that held two lamps, a cup, a loom weight and a bone die;other items in Room (6-88) included a *pyxis* lid, a *krater*, a miniature cup and a red-figure vessel. In the interior Room (6-87) were a bowl, cups, a jug, miniature vessels, loom weights and coins. Although there is no firm evidence for cooking and washing in these rooms, there are a number of personal items and the quantity of these, along with the lack of any commercial or industrial activity suggest that this could have been a residential area.

The last unit consists of the porch and court, with two attached areas, Room (6-85) and (6-82). The court contained a number of items relating to food storage, preparation and serving; a bronze finger ring with an engraved bezel was found too. The porch area contained mostly serving pottery, some of which was red-figured. Room (6-85) contained no catalogued finds; Room (6-82) was self-enclosed and contained only a nail. Apart from the use of unit (6-83), (6-84) and (6-86), there is no real indication of industrial or commercial activity in the building. It is likely that the spaces were predominantly residential.

House C

The rooms in House C were divided into a number of interrelated units (see **Plan 9**, p. 177). The entrance, Room (6-63), and Corridor (6-59) provide access to three rooms. Rooms (6-61) and (6-64) contained no finds worthy of note; the Court (6-63), (6-59) and Room (6-60) held a range of items connected with food preparation and storage, such as a hopper mill—a mill for grinding grain—made from dacite stone and a *pithos*, as well as pottery connected with food storage and drinking. The quantity of items was small and it is difficult to see any purpose, either purely industrial or purely residential, for the spaces—it is possible that these were simply storage places. The courtyard area contained a porch and a number of storage vessels as well as items for eating and drinking. The unit of rooms to the east of the court, Rooms (6-57) and (6-58), were not fully excavated and so could offer no indication as to their use.

The remaining unit, Porch (6-54) and Rooms (6-55) and (6-56), offered a much more complex picture. The porch area had red plaster on the walls and contained two amphorae, a drinking cup and some coins and nails. Room (6-55) could not be completely excavated and was also quite low in finds. In contrast to the other two spaces in the suite, Room (6-56) had a large quantity of pottery, including a number of pots associated with the serving and consumption of food and drink. There were also personal items: a *louterion* rim, a *lekanis-pyxis*, an *amphoriskos*, a loom weight, a ring, a pruning knife, a bronze earring and part of a chain or another bronze earring. These items are traditionally linked to women, but here they appear to be part of a discard assemblage. Although this suggests that women were present in the building, we cannot say where.

House D

House D appears to be subdivided into three distinct units, two of which have their own entrance to the street (see **Plan 10**, p. 178). The first unit consists of Rooms (6-26) to (6-29). The courtyard area, (6-26), had a plaster pavement on its western side that may have been connected to work activities, either public or private. A range of different vessels was found here, including items for storage, food preparation and eating. There were also signs of residential activities through the presence of a griddle for cooking, and a large number of personal items were found here, among them a feeder (a vessel designed to feed a baby), a fishhook, a decorative plaque, bronze earrings and a bronze ring. Room (6-29) was a porch area opening off the court into two rear rooms, (6-27) and (6-28). The porch area contained a plaster platform with a limestone press bed for extracting olive oil. It also held a *pithos*, a cup and bowl and a griddle for cooking. Room (6-27) had only an amphora and a strainer, and Room (6-28) had two rings, a sickle blade and a pink cylinder seal. Taking all the evidence for this portion of the building into account, it appears to offer us evidence of residence and small-scale economic activity. The items found in this section also seem to indicate that the space, at some point, had a male and female presence, as well as a baby.

The second portion of the house consists of rooms (6-30) to (6-36). Room (6-30) contains another large hearth, measuring roughly 65cm x 75cm and open to its south-east side with a perimeter constructed of mud brick. The hearth almost fills the available area and is clearly the central feature of the room, but as the room is very small and not enclosed, it bears no resemblance to the spatial arrangements of the hearth rooms at Olynthus. The hearth was packed with ceramic debris, including red-figure items related to eating and drinking, which were deposited after the building was abandoned. Room (6-31), adjoining the hearth room, appears to have been a courtyard area, offering entrance from the street; this area had very few fragments. The court gave entry to rooms (6-32), (6-33) and (6-34), although the latter room could not be excavated. Rooms (6-32) and (6-33) offered little insight into the roles that they played in the building, containing only a few amphorae and cups. The final unit was a series of three interlocking rooms (6-35a, 6-35b and 6-36) at the back of the house to which access was gained through the court and porch. These three rooms contained large quantities of pottery related to dining, drinking and food preparation. A griddle for cooking and a spool and needle were found here, as well as personal items such as two *strigils*, a razor, a bronze ring and a bronze earring or pendant. The absence of economic activity and the presence of personal items and evidence of domestic activity supports the notion that this portion of House D was used for residence.

House E

House E can also be divided into three separate areas, each with its own entrance from the street (see **Plan 10**, p. 178). The portion in the west of the building, Rooms (6-11) to (6-13) is a central court with two rooms to the north and south. This section could not be completely excavated and the finds were sparse and relatively uninformative. The central portion of House E consisted of an L-shaped court, rooms opening off it and an area of rooms towards the back of the house and entered via a porch type area. The court (6-19/20) contained a marble *perirrhanterion* rim—a vessel associated with washing—items for serving and consuming drink, for preparing, cooking and serving food and a number of loom weights. Room (6-18) held vessels for cooking and drinking. The porch area had drinking cups, storage vessels, loom weights, various items for preparing and serving food and drink and miniatures.

The rooms at the rear of the house consist of an access room, (6-23), leading into two further rooms, (6-25) and (6-16). The latter room offers exclusive access to the small space (6-17). The entrance space had drinking, eating and storage vessels, as well as a grinding slab; Room (6-25) had mostly amphorae and loom weights; and Room (6-16) had a brazier and a loom weight. Room (6-17) had no finds but was covered in plaster and had a plaster shelf with a bowl and a base for a *louterion* at the centre of the room—it was almost certainly concerned with washing activities. A number of personal items were also present in these spaces, including a slate pendant, a needle and the figurine of a bird. Our last unit consists of Rooms (6-21) and (6-22), which held bowls, cups, a *pyxis*, an incense burner and a *louterion* rim fragment, again connected to washing. These two rooms offer an image of residence rather than industry or commerce.

Observations

Athenian texts offer us the best view of family life, although they do not always offer us a clear view of houses. Using archaeological evidence is more complex: although we can identify areas of residence within the buildings of classical cities, we cannot see the social status or relationships between the residents. It is easy to formulate an archaeological model for identifying a family—in practice it is not so easy to apply. The material evidence from classical houses is patchy and must be examined on an individual basis, and is further complicated by the style of excavation and the quality of excavation reporting. It is difficult to pinpoint a specific area where a family may have resided in private buildings. Equally, we have problems in using evidence of residence to identify houses. At Athens and Olynthus, residence is only one of many functions performed by spaces in the private buildings. As a result, residents may have been present in only a small portion of a larger, multi-use building. The family home may be no more than one or two rooms. The buildings at Halieis appear to be more discrete, with their internal spaces divided into work and living areas. The fact that these are contained within the same building and are small in scale is persuasive evidence that the same resident group may have used them. The buildings at Halieis bear more resemblance to the modern concept of a house, but unfortunately it is difficult to know exactly who the users of the buildings were. We know that the house was the primary locus of family life and played an essential role in the classical city but the importance of the link between family and house shown in texts is not always revealed by studies of material remains.

CHAPTER 4

WORKING FROM HOME
HOUSE AND ECONOMY

I n the modern 'new' cities of the USA and the UK, industrial
  activity tends to be pushed to the margins. The noise and
smell that industrial activity produces does not sit well with the
other roles that a city plays, such as habitation or commerce.
Commercial spaces are more flexible: offices can be found in central
urban areas as well as at the margins, shops are concentrated at
the centre but are also threaded though the neighbourhoods of
the city. This clear structure is not apparent in the classical city;
indeed, we have already seen that evidence of production and
commerce are intertwined with houses and religious structures.
They can also occur alongside evidence of habitation within
a single building. In this chapter, we will turn to look in more
detail at the material and textual evidence for economic activity
in the buildings in Athens, Olynthus and Halieis. Using texts,
we will explore the economic behaviour of the Athenian family
and assess the range of activities carried out by the Athenian
household. We will then turn to material evidence from the
buildings that have been identified as houses at our sites and
consider what types of economic activities took place within
them. Our aim is to consider the relationship between economic
behaviour and domesticity, to assess the range of activities that
could co-exist in 'houses', to investigate the connections between

work and residence within the buildings and, in so doing, to gain a fuller understanding of the role that house and household played in the urban economy.

Working in Athens: the view from texts

Athenian texts contain many references to the economic activities performed by or within households. In order to survive, the Athenian household needed to provide for its members, to attain a degree of self-sufficiency. The family and other household members had to have their most basic needs met; they had to be clothed and to be fed. It is no surprise, therefore, that the act most commonly associated with the Athenian house is the production of textiles. Many texts refer to textile manufacture and indicate that this work was the primary responsibility of the women in the house. In the ideal house of Ischomachus, his wife is responsible for making textiles and supervising the slaves who carry out the weaving (Xenophon *Oeconomicus* 7.6, 7.36). Plato notes that women control the shuttles and wool-work, and there is a loom in the house where Chrysis lives (Plato *Laws* 805E; Menander *Samia* 233). The link between women and the production of cloth and clothes is exploited for comic effect by Aristophanes: the women in *Lysistrata* will solve the tangled political problems of the city just as they smooth and untangle wool (Aristophanes *Lysistrata* 574–86). Most of the references to household textile production appear to relate to family needs, but there are indications that the enterprise had a commercial element—a surplus is produced for sale. In *Memorabilia*, Socrates reveals that even wealthy households would produce a surplus of textiles and sell them to overcome times of economic difficulty (Xenophon *Memorabilia* 2.7.12). The plaintiff Euxitheus states that, despite being citizens, his family are sellers of headbands (Demosthenes 57.30–1). Texts also mention the dyeing of and cleansing of cloth (Plato *Republic* 429D–30B; Theophrastus *Characters* 10.14). There is no indication in any of these passages that special buildings were required for these activities; the whole economic production of cloth and clothes could be performed by household members and could take place in their private space, their house.

The household and its members also needed to be fed, yet the textual evidence for food production within the household is scarce. This is not surprising: the settlement of Athens comprised not only the urban centre, the city itself, but also Attica, the land around it. We are told by philosophers, historians and playwrights alike that the land around Athens was fertile and produced enough crops to sustain the Athenian population (Plato *Critias* 110E–111D; Xenophon *Revenues* 1.2-8; Aristophanes fr. 569.1–8, 'Seasons'). The citizens of Athens did not need to pursue agricultural practices inside the city; they could use their lands in the Attic countryside to produce food. Some of the wealthier city residents may have used their city properties for food production: in a legal speech by Demosthenes, the speaker mentions his smallholding near the Hippodrome (47.53–4). We are told that the plot has a garden and, although no reference is made to the production of food, we cannot rule out the possibility that the land was used in this way. However, for the most part, Athenian residents would have obtained food from the markets, and in order to buy food—or any other necessary items—they needed to indulge in activities that made money. Economic practices were therefore an essential feature of city and household life at Athens.

In order to make money, Athenians carried out a wide range of commercial and industrial activities. Yet, despite the importance and necessity of work, texts suggest that the Athenians may have had a contradictory attitude to their endeavours. The ideal mode of employment for a male citizen was to be a gentleman farmer (Xenophon *Oeconomicus* 5.1). Those who worked in *banausic* occupations, at the behest of an employer, are criticized by philosophers and historians (Aristotle *Politics* 1278A; Xenophon *Oeconomicus* 4.2–3); the family of the politician Cleon were mocked for being tanners (Aristophanes *Knights* 43–5). Trade and production were seen as being unsuitable types of activities for citizens (Aristotle *Rhetoric* 1367A). This censure does not appear to have impeded the opportunities available to citizens, though; an involvement in production and trade did not prevent Cleon from participating in the political arena. The disapproval of philosophers also appears to have had little real effect on constraining the range of productive activity undertaken by citizens. Citizens owned the leases on the mines and were content to adopt managerial or ownership roles in trading. Athens was a very large city: without cobblers, dung collectors, farmers and administrators it could not function. Texts show that the citizens themselves performed these acts. In *Memorabilia*, Socrates offers the information that:

> Nausikides not only supports himself and his slaves by manufacturing flour, but also keeps large quantities of cattle and pigs. And, in spite of this, he often has so much to spare that he undertakes costly liturgies; Kyrebus feeds his whole family well and lives in luxury by baking bread, Demeas of Kollytus by making cloaks, Menon by making women's garments . . . (Xenophon *Memorabilia* 2.7.6)

It is clear that the citizens engaged in all manner of trade and employment in Athens and did not allow reservations about it to get in the way of their livelihood.

Although texts can tell us about the type of work undertaken, they offer us little indication of where work was performed. The father of Lysias is described as owning a shield factory, but we have no knowledge of where it was and what it looked like (Lysias 12.17–20). In the court case 'Against Olympiadorus', the deceased's property is divided in two, with a business and a building given to each of the individuals concerned (Demosthenes 48.12): one man receives a building and slaves who make sackcloth, the other receives a building and slaves who grind colours for paint. But neither of these passages offers any clue as to the location or appearance of the place of manufacture or sale. Texts often indicate that slave production units could be inherited on the death of the original owner. As well as the example above, Demosthenes mentions the inheritance of two workshops, one with knife makers and one with couch makers (27.9). Aeschines reveals that Timarchus inherited nine or ten slaves who were skilled shoemakers and their overseer (Aeschines 1.97); each of them paid a fee to Timarchus to allow them to profit from their labours. These fee-paying slaves probably worked at a place away from the residence of Timarchus, and for financial reasons it is likely that they lived in their workplace.

The modern city separates most places of work from homes: an individual goes out to work and returns home at the end of the day. This type of behaviour is more applicable in classical Athens when work involves the sale of products. In *Women at the Thesmophoria* a widow describes how she makes chaplets and sells them in the myrtle market to support herself and her children (Aristophanes *Women at the Thesmophoria* 448). However, although it seems logical to assume that buying and selling was concentrated in markets, this does not mean that the sellers had stalls in the market; they may have sold their products through traders with shops in the city or even from the place where they lived and produced the items, from their homes around the Agora. In *Lysistrata*, the tavern keeper could conceivably serve wine in the premises where he resides (Aristophanes *Lysistrata* 456–9), and prostitutes could live and work in the same building (Xenophon *Memorabilia* 3.11.4). This reinforces the observations that we have made to date: there was no differentiation between the buildings where people worked and the buildings where they lived.

In the case of service industries, it is highly likely that home and work were closely connected. Many service activities require only a room. Pasion is a banker who hires out his bank—his work did not require a special place (Demosthenes 36.4). Aeschines and Plato both mention schools, but we know nothing of what a school looked like (Aeschines 1.9–10; Plato *Lysis* 208D). Schools only required a room and chairs—they did not need a specific architecture, and may have mimicked a house in appearance. In *Clouds* Strepsiades is able to point out a building that is a school while he is in his bedroom (Aristophanes *Clouds* 91–2), which suggests that houses and schools could exist side by side in the same urban district. Doctors and medical practitioners also worked from private buildings; there is no indication that their buildings had a special architecture or can even be identified by examining the material remains. In some cases, the medical worker came into the house of the patient: in *Women at the Thesmophoria* a midwife comes to the home to deliver the baby (Aristophanes *Women at the Thesmophoria* 505). It is also possible that the teachers of girls and very young children may well have come into the family house to work.

The house played a direct role in the urban rental market (Osborne 1988). As only a citizen could own land, and non-Athenian Greeks, *metics* and freedmen needed a place to stay, Athenians made money by renting out properties and land.

Aristotle records that the property of orphans was rented out on their behalf by the state through a supervising archon (Aristotle *Constitution of Athens* 56.6–7), and Isaeus notes that Chiron rented out one of his properties in the city near the Temple of Dionysus Limineia (Isaeus 8.35). Land rental could result in a high turnover of residents. A speech by Lysias records that a single plot of land was let to Callistratus for two years, then to Demetrius for a year, then to Alcias, a freedman, for another year and finally to Proteus for three years (Lysias 7.9–10). The passage by Aeschines quoted in Chapter 2 indicates that an individual did not have to rent a whole property but could take a room or rooms there (Aeschines 1.123–4). We know also that Philoneus and Philondas only used or resided in part of a building (Antiphon 1.14; Demosthenes 49.26). Again as we have seen in Chapter 2, certain buildings or *synoikia* were allocated for leasing to a number of groups or individuals. These could be used for a range of uses, including industrial, commercial or residential. Their profitability is indicated by their use in lieu of cash for dowries (Isaeus 5.27).

Working from home in classical Athens

Texts offer us a view of work and workers but our view is restricted according to the interests of the author and the needs of the narrative. Even our passage about the flexible nature of space and changes in spatial terminology that result from this comes from a speech whose purpose is to denigrate the name and social status of the defendant Timarchus, rather than describe his living arrangements (Aeschines 1.123–4). In contrast, archaeology offers us a more direct view of the economic activities taking place in 'houses'. In Athens, the buildings in the valley between the Areopagus and the Hill of the Nymphs contained evidence of many different 'heavy' trades such as marble working, bronze casting and even dyeing, which resulted in excavators naming the area the 'Industrial District'. The houses in the Street of the Marble Workers were littered with chips of marble, showing that sculptors worked there. In Building H there was a sculptor's workshop that was liberally covered with marble chips; Building G had layers of marble dust in the court and a block of marble partially sculpted into a herm, and another herm arm was found in the Poros Building, a building usually identified as a prison. In fact, the excavators noted that the greatest evidence of marble dust and chips came from G, H, K and the Poros Building, suggesting that the Poros Building may have played a part in the creation or sale of marble artefacts. A large hearth with evidence of metalworking was found in the south-east corner of the courtyard of House D (see **Plan 2**, p. 174). It was bordered by thin stones and tiles set on the edges of its north and west sides and floored with square tiles. Ashes and charcoal were present in the interior, while shapeless slugs of iron and bronze were found in the ashes and around the edge of the hearth, indicating that metalworking took place here. House F had three vats lined with waterproof cement suggesting that the occupiers were working with or soaking material in liquid. The central space in between the vats was a terrazzo floor, easy to clean, and there were no stains, no signs of dyeing, and no grindstones. There were many pieces of animal bones, implying that the users made bone tools. In all of these cases, there is no indication that the activities are in any way separated from areas of residence. The rooms within the building open onto the court and there is nothing to suggest that access is restricted.

There is also evidence for craftwork in the buildings around the Agora. The House of Simon appears to have housed a cobbler's workshop. Hobnails and other paraphernalia were spread throughout the building. The remains of a potter's establishment was uncovered beneath the eastern edge of the Panatheniac Way, and another was destroyed and covered over by the construction of the Stoa of Zeus on the Kolonos Agoraios. The archaeological evidence indicates that these workshops were in buildings that had little difference from those identified as houses. A deep shaft excavated in this area contained waste from a number of potters' establishments that may have been operating nearby, and a concentration of coroplasts' clay moulds and plaques were found in the remains on the north and west slopes of the Areopagus. We also find many moulds for the making of figurines in buildings that have been identified as houses or in wells in residential areas. It is possible that households may have produced such items for an agent or for sale in a shop owned by another. The small scale of industry found in some buildings may show their participation in a cottage or franchise type industry.

While we can find evidence of work in residential buildings, it is extremely difficult to tell who is doing the work: women may have worked in coroplasty, or at furnaces; citizen workers may have made marble stele or dyed textiles. Equally, we cannot tell whether the worker was free or a slave. The people in House D who worked at the furnace and lived in the rooms may well have been slaves, with their owners living elsewhere. Despite Athens being a slave-owning society, we have very little evidence to identify areas of work associated with slaves in the buildings of the city and its surrounding countryside. Slaves do not bring their pottery or jewellery with them from their homelands when they become slaves. They have nothing and have to use the items they are given (Morris 1998). As a result, we cannot distinguish them as separate racial or ethnic groups in the material record. We may use the evidence to tell us if women were present, or to assess if residential activities were carried out in a space, but we cannot tell if the user of the space was a citizen or a slave.

Within the city we know that many traders sold their wares around the Agora, yet there are no indications that shops occupied a certain section of the city. It seems likely that many products were sold where they were made. The shoes made by the cobbler in the House of Simon could have been sold on his premises; a client of the marble worker needed only to come to the workshop to collect or commission a piece. In House C, Room 12 was separated from the other spaces and had a single entrance onto the street, and the excavator, Young, suggests that this room was used as a shop, yet there is no evidence of any type of production in the remainder of the building (1951: 207; see **Plan 2**, p. 174). In this case, the space may have been used by a separate group to sell products. Inscriptions make reference to taverns, and the remains of a wine shop was situated near the gate of the Kerameikos (Lawall 2000: 76), but these establishments had no need to consist of more than a room or two in a larger building. We may also see a more commercial role in some of the formal dining rooms. Just outside the room with a dolphin mosaic in the Central House on the north-east slopes of the Areopagus was a cistern packed with pottery for eating, drinking and serving (see **Plan 1**, p. 173). The large quantities present here suggest commercial rather than domestic activities. Similarly, the size of the dining room in Menander Street and the absence of any evidence for a building around it could indicate that the room and its outer chamber made up a complete single building—a building for available for hire by interested parties.

Working from home in Olynthus

There is plentiful evidence for the role of Olynthian 'houses' in economic activities (Cahill 2002: 223–88). This includes signs of agricultural, industrial and commercial pursuits as well as activities related to service industries and possibly to the financial industry. With regard to agricultural work we have evidence of processing and storage within the buildings at the site: there are cement platforms and floors, which appear to have been used for crushing grapes or olives in A vi 8 and A vi 10. and A xi 10, and Building A6 contained twelve grindstones. There is no indication that the grindstones were manufactured at this location, and therefore it seems likely that they were used to grind wheat or corn to make flour on a scale that provided for more than just one household. There is also evidence of large-scale storage in the Villa of Good Fortune, the House of Twin Erotes and the Villa of the Bronzes. The signs of large-scale storage in the villa houses contrast with the smaller scale of storage found in buildings within the city walls. This may be for practical reasons: the buildings in the Villa Section may simply have been closest to the agricultural areas and so it was easier to transport the goods to them. However, the use of corner rooms adjacent to the street and with their own separate entrances in the three buildings mentioned above may imply that the storage was part of a commercial enterprise; this could have consisted of the sale of agricultural products or their use in activities within the building itself, such as dining in the Villa of Good Fortune.

There is also evidence of industrial and manufacturing activities within the buildings on the North Hill. Products and debris from sculpture and stonecutting are present in two of the buildings on Row A. The location of these buildings may reflect a need to ensure easy access to the supply of raw materials, but it may also show an awareness of the need to reduce the disruption that such activities are capable of causing within the community. Row A is positioned against the West Wall at the site, it is furthest from the villa houses and also at the very edge of the settlement. This position would minimize the noise and dust entering the settlement. The buildings of Row A are also different in shape as a result of their urban position. Rather than being square, they are long, although in some cases, their full length has not been excavated. In Building A5, portable altars, stone reliefs, grave stele, *louters* and unworked blocks of stone were present in the court, Room (d). This space was situated at the back of the house, against the wall and furthest away from the buildings in the grid and Villa Section. Building A10 contained signs of architectural stone working, portable altars and unworked stone. The majority of this evidence was found in the court, Room (k), the remainder was in Room (h), which might have been a storeroom or sales room. Room (h) was positioned at the back of the building and the court was positioned in the middle, divided from Avenue A by a layer of rooms. The length of the buildings, the placement of the activities within them and the width of Avenue A enhanced the spatial barrier between the stone working and the houses in the grid section.

Other signs of industrial manufacture are dotted through the buildings on the North Hill. There is evidence for smelting in C x 5, which is situated in the far north and near the city wall. Again, it is possible that the smell, noise and heat from this type of activity may have been pushed to the outer limits of the settlement. The building has a very large court, which contained a sunken area surrounded by blocks of Poros stone, fragments of lead and a mould for making sling bullets. There are shallow stone troughs in the court and in Room (f), which may have been connected with the activities here. Building B vi 10 also contained a bronze mould for making arrowheads. There is no sign of fires or furnaces at these buildings and it is possible that the buildings were used for finishing products made elsewhere.

Just as there is little evidence for industrial-size fires at Olynthus, neither is there evidence for a kiln, which is particularly significant for the work of coroplasts. There are many terracotta figurines at Olynthus and pottery made from local materials, but without a kiln, these could not have been fired at the site and must have been made elsewhere and either brought in for finishing or brought in fully complete, for sale. Despite this, there are many moulds present in the buildings at the site. At B i 5 around thirteen moulds were found in Room (i). This is the largest concentration at the site; in other buildings such as the House of the Twin Erotes, only one or two moulds were found. It is possible that figurines were not produced at any single site, and that instead, individuals or groups paid for the use of a mould, filled it and allowed the clay to dry before the moulds were collected in a group for firing. This would help to explain the differences in quality that appear to exist between some of the figurines, and also the number of figurines at Olynthus that were made from the same mould.

Although the households in Athenian texts prized the ideal of self-sufficiency, urban life required the production of a surplus and this appears to have equally been the case at Olynthus. There is evidence for the manufacture of household necessities such as food and clothes. A unit of rooms in House A viii 8 appears to have operated as a bakery: Room (j) had a cobbled floor, which was covered in ash and had large amounts of cooking pottery; the room opposite, Room (f), had evidence of food preparation with a big stone trough containing two basins and a large stone mortar, and fragments of coarse pottery, ashes and other evidence of fire were also present in this room. A building on the East Spur Hill (E.S.H. 4) contained two identical 'kitchen complex' areas: one was positioned within the main body of the building (Rooms b, c, d), while the other was situated adjacent to Street i and could be entered from it (Rooms h, h', i). Room (h) contained a stone mortar, and a number of grindstones were also present in the building. Room (j), a cement-floored workroom with a catch basin, was also positioned next to Room (h), and so it seems likely that this area was used for non-household food preparation. The large cooking pits in A viii 3 and the House of Many Colours were also designed to cater for large-scale catering needs and could indicate the presence of commercial enterprises in these buildings (see **Plan 6**, p. 176). There is evidence that textile manufacture took place in A viii 7 and A viii 9. These two buildings had been joined together and 247 loom weights, the largest concentration at Olynthus, were found in Room (d), the porch area, while another fifty loom weights were found in the adjacent room (b). This number of loom weights suggests that up to twelve looms could have been set up here. While we cannot be certain that these were not to provide clothes for a very large family group, it is an exceptional deposit and probably indicates manufacture rather than private consumption.

In contrast with the evidence from Athens, economic activities at Olynthus appear to have taken place in more visibly separated spaces within the buildings. The crushing platforms in A vi 8, A vi 10 and A xi 10 are all in discrete rooms that are connected to the court but to no other room in the building. In A viii 8, the 'bakery' is a separated unit of three rooms with its own entrance onto the street. In A viii 3 and the House of Many Colours, the cooking areas are separated from other spaces and are part of self-contained units. Even where activities take place in the court, there is some evidence that the effect on other spaces in the building is minimized as far as possible: the court of A5 is at the rear of the building; the court in A10 is not positioned centrally but lies in against the eastern wall of the building, while the main body of rooms lies against the western wall. As a result, we must acknowledge the possibility that the economic activity is being performed not by members of a discrete household but by different individuals who own or lease rooms in the buildings. This idea is reinforced by a study of A iv 5 and A iv 7, two buildings that operated as separate entities until the western half of A iv 7 was sold to the owner of A vi 5, who appears to have used it for economic activities in connection with coin manufacture. There would appear to be no bar on the acquisition and use of spaces in the buildings for non-domestic purposes.

There is also evidence that the buildings were used as points of sale. Cahill suggests that the open area to the south of Block iv was an agora, a marketplace where such sales could be made (2002: 32). While this is a possibility, there is little in the area to suggest that it performed the same functions as the Athenian Agora or other agoras found in classical Greek cities. As at Athens, when buying an altar or a loaf of bread, the purchaser could simply walk into the place of manufacture, select the required item, pay on the spot and take it home. Similarly, the small-scale evidence of storage in the buildings at the site might also indicate that this was the point of sale. In these cases a separate shop would not be required. Nevertheless, all items sold by a seller rather than a manufacturer, such as clothes and pottery, would require a separate place where they were displayed. Many of the buildings facing onto Avenue B, such as A iv 9, have rooms that are separated from the internal spaces and have their own entrances onto the street (see **Fig. 5**). It is possible that these spaces are shops, and this would appear to be confirmed by the high concentration of coins found in the rooms, suggesting that they may have been involved in commercial activity

(Cahill 2002: 266). Building A iv 9 contained ninety-nine coins, most of which were spread through its three separated rooms. It is perhaps possible to see Avenue B as the main shopping street—it certainly produced more coins than any other area excavated in the city. This evidence raises an interesting point: if Olynthus was not democratic but ruled by an oligarchy or social elite, then it would have been a dangerous move to permit the existence of an agora that allowed the residents to meet and discuss community and political issues. It would be better to disperse such areas through the city and prevent large gatherings of citizens. Hence, a shopping street would be a necessity and an agora was not needed.

Communities also need spaces to accommodate service industries, such as schools, doctors' rooms or social meeting places. Schools and doctors' rooms do not need much beyond a room and some simple furniture. It is interesting that a large statue of Asclepius, god of doctors, stood outside the formal

5 *Shop units in Building A iv 9, Olynthus (photo J.E. Morgan)*

dining room in B vi 7 (see **Plan 5**, p. 175); the cult of Asclepius required an individual to sleep in the sanctuary in order to be healed, and so the borders in this room may have supported couches for sleeping, not dining. The separation of this room and the corridor and room opposite from the rest of the house highlights the isolation of the area—this part of B vi 7 may have operated as a healing sanctuary. There are also rooms and buildings that appear to be more suited to social behaviour than to domestic behaviour. Building B v 1 had a highly decorated mosaic in its bordered room and had approximately twenty-eight coins spread through it, perhaps indicating that this room was available for hire, or a place where people spent money. The layout of A xi 9 with its large elaborate court and cement-bordered room to the north may hint at a commercial rather than private use for this building. The elaborate decoration and layout of the Villa of Good Fortune is not replicated by any other building at the site—it is not difficult to see it as a hostelry or entertainment venue.

Working from home in Halieis

The main type of work undertaken in the buildings of Halieis was agricultural. It is possible that a wider range of work was undertaken in the buildings of the town or that certain types of activity focused on certain parts of the town—we do not know, as not all of the urban space could be excavated (Ault 2005). Halieis was a small town; it may not have needed the diverse range of economic activities that we see in larger sites. The land around Halieis was fertile and productive, and it is perhaps no surprise that the evidence from the buildings shows a bias towards agricultural and food production. House D was involved in the processing of olives: the olives were crushed in the court and taken to Room (6-29), where there was a plaster platform with a limestone press bed for extracting the olive oil. In some houses we find installations that may have been used for industrial purposes. In House A, Room (6-83) had a plastered platform with a cobbled kerb and plaster on the walls (see **Plan 8**, p. 177), with two storage jars or *pithoi* sunk into the platform. The arrangements hint at a wet activity but we cannot say what. Similarly in House D, Room (6-32) had a plastered area. In the majority of cases, evidence is on a much smaller scale, which could relate to the food production for a household or could be part of a spread of activity—a form of cottage industry, with collection from an agent. Grindstones are often found in the houses, as in Houses A, D and E; House E also had a whetstone. There are signs of storage in the form of *pithoi* in House C Room (6-60).

There is some evidence for commercial behaviour in Halieis. In House E, Rooms (6-21) and (6-22) formed a unit that was separated from the house, which could have been shops, as in House C at Athens. The evidence from House 7 strongly supports the idea that the building played a commercial role (see **Plan 7**, p. 176). While there were signs of at least 824 vessels within the property, a further deposit of 754 vessels was found in the street outside Rooms (7-9/7-10). Room (7-9) was a formal dining area, and its presence in the house, alongside the large cooking hearth in (7-16/7-17), suggests that food and drink were being provided on a commercial basis. Despite having the largest area of the houses at Halieis, House 7 had the least evidence for personal items and domestic behaviour. Although Room (7-12) was identified as a possible living space by the excavator Ault, he acknowledged that the presence of a circle marked out with stones might be connected to gaming activities (Ault 2005). It would not be unreasonable to view the whole building as a business concerned with hospitality and entertainment. The formal dining rooms in Area T and Area 5 may also have been available for hire or might have played a similar commercial role while the hearth in House D could have been used for cooking on a scale wider than domestic.

There is an interesting pattern to the spatial arrangements within the private buildings of Halieis. The internal spaces appear to be divided, with work areas separated from other areas but still remaining linked and accessible within the same building. The court is used as an access space rather than a control space, providing a link between the workspaces and the more private spaces of the building. In House 7, the court, dining room and hearth constitute a unit, separated from the rooms in the north-east of the house. In House A, the room with the plaster platform is separated from other spaces in the building. In House C, the areas that are connected with storage or work are in the south of the building while the other rooms are in the north. Both of the separated halves of House D followed the same pattern, with work areas in the south and more private rooms screened behind a porch area in the north. The same pattern was followed in the middle section of House E. Yet the separation is not absolute: although areas of work and residence are kept apart, they are still in areas that are interconnected.

Observations

The range and specialization of economic activity present at our sites increases in proportion to the size of the urban settlement. At Halieis evidence consists mostly of agricultural processing alongside basic economic activities such as the minting of coins and possible facilities for private functions or visitors to the town. In our larger cities of Athens and Olynthus, the

range of economic activities is much wider. There is evidence
for manufacturing, commercial, financial, industry and leisure
activities. The more complex a society becomes, the greater its
needs and the more specialized its economic activities become.

The activities take place in buildings that also contain
evidence of domestic and religious activity, which reinforces the
inappropriate nature of the constant application of the term
'house' to these buildings. The relationship between work and
residence differs at each site. At Halieis the small scale of the
economic activity, the use of the court as an access and dividing
space and the integration of work into the structure of the
main building are more indicative of the space being utilized by
one group; it does seem appropriate to view these buildings as
having a primarily residential function and the economic activity
as being linked to the resident group. In Athens, our ability to
read the evidence is hampered by the style of the excavation:
residential evidence has not been fully reported or published, and
as a result we can see economic activity but cannot tell exactly
how it was integrated into buildings with evidence of domestic
activities. In the West House excavated on the north-east slopes
of the Areopagus, the unit with the cement-lined tank is situated
in the furthest reaches of the building, in a section that opens
off the court. It is difficult to read this use of space—we may
be looking at a building used by a single social group or at a
collection of separately owned or hired spaces. The evidence here
contrasts with the many entrances in the housing block on the
north slopes of the Areopagus, which more clearly suggests that
different groups may have lived and worked in sections of the
buildings.

At Olynthus, there is more evidence for divisions between
suites of rooms within the buildings and many of these units
had separate entrances to the street. This arrangement of space

seems more suited to the use of a building by different groups and for different purposes. However, there is a great deal of variation in the material from the Olynthian buildings. Some, such as A viii 8, have evidence of production and no evidence of domestic behaviour; here industry and religion appear to mix. In A iv 9, the commercial spaces are clearly divorced from the residential spaces. In A2 and A10, there is a single street entrance and clear evidence of production but, as the buildings were excavated at the earliest stages of the project, the data on artefacts is sparse and we have little way of knowing if these building were also residences. The processes of production and distribution and commercial activity in the classical city were not controlled by businesses, as in modern cities of the USA and the UK; they were much smaller in scale and controlled by individuals or small groups, such as families. Economic activities did not need large, separate premises but could be woven into the urban landscape, taking space in the residences of the practitioners or in hired rooms belonging to other urban buildings. While the activities found in urban buildings indicate that they did not have a wholly domestic use, it is reasonable to assume that the control of economic activity was certainly in the hands of the household, even if it did not always occur in their own discrete places of residence.

CHAPTER 5

GENDER IDEOLOGY AND THE CLASSICAL HOUSE

One area of scholarship where the classical house plays a vitally important role in an ideological and physical sense is in the field of gender relations. Evidence from texts indicates that men and women used separate areas in the classical house. Authors mention that men could gather in an area designated specifically for their use, indicated by the term *andron* or *andronitis* (men's room or men's place), while women could be present in a similarly designated area, the *gunaikon* or *gunaikonitis* (women's room or women's place). The aim of this chapter is therefore twofold. We will look at the language and practice of domestic gender division in Athenian texts from the classical period to try to understand how and why the words are used in relation to the house. Then we will examine the material evidence for gender division in the houses of Athens, Olynthus and Halieis to consider how far their architecture offers an image that reinforces or rejects the view presented in the texts. To what extent was the classical house used to express and reinforce urban gender ideology?

A woman's place in classical Athens

We begin by looking at the information that texts offer about female separation and seclusion. Is it a myth or do texts indicate that it had a concrete basis? Texts inform us that the action of confining women in the house reinforced the ideology of citizenship by allowing the family to maintain the purity and reputation of citizen wives and thus the legitimacy of children. This is a requirement not to be underestimated in a society where legitimate citizens had all the rights and non-citizens had nothing and were nothing by comparison. Gender separation is equated with purity and set up as a model of correct behaviour by women in all manner of texts. Andromache states that, as a new wife: 'First of all I stayed indoors and put aside any desire for going out—which gets one a bad name whether or not one deserves it' (Euripides *Trojan Women* 643–56). A character in a fragment by the comic poet Menander notes: 'For the free woman, the street door is the limit imposed by custom' (fr. 815). In a passage by Xenophon, Ischomachus' wife is told that she will have to stay inside and take care of the stores and the servants (Xenophon *Oeconomicus* 7.35). While these passages reinforce the notion that gender separation was an ideological construct, others indicate that the division had an architectural basis—women were restricted to a specific area or room within the house. In the speech 'Against Simon', the orator notes that the accused broke into his house and entered the *gunaikon* occupied by his sister and nieces (Lysias 3.6); the house of Euphiletos has male and female areas, an *andronitis* and a *gunaikonitis* (Lysias 1.9.1–4), and in Aristophanes' play *Women at the Thesmophoria* (786–91, 414–17) the ladies note that they are forbidden to leave the house, or even to show themselves at windows and that to keep them in the house their men have put seals and bars on the *gunaikonitis*.

These textual examples suggest that the *gunaikon* is a specific area, capable of being clearly identified and locked. Unfortunately, they tell us little about the *gunaikon*'s appearance or location. When Euphiletos describes the organization of his house, he places the *gunaikon* on an upper storey: 'And so first, gentlemen . . . my little house is on two floors with the upper being equal to the lower, with the women's space above and men's below (Lysias 1.9.1–4). Classical texts suggest that upper storeys offered protection to women—female activities are often linked to the roof of the house, as at the festival of the Adonia (Plato *Phaedrus* 276B; Menander *Samia* 35–50; Aristophanes *Lysistrata* 387–96). In Aristophanes' *Acharnians* (262) when Dicaeopolis wishes to begin his festival, he sends his wife up to the roof to watch. Yet the roof is not only used on religious occasions: in Euripides' *Phoenician Women* (22–102), Antigone climbs to the roof of the palace to view the Argive army. Roofs offered women a protected site for their activities; they are part of the household, part of the city, but out of reach. Texts do not tell us that the roof or upper storeys were seen as female space on a permanent basis, but they do suggest that, when necessary, upper storeys could operate as a form of *gunaikon*, a woman's place that enabled them to participate in Athenian life yet to be separated and inviolate.

Although upper storeys could offer a location for women's activities, it would be somewhat specious to claim that all references to the *gunaikon* are references to the roof, as no upper storeys of the classical Greek house survive. We can neither prove nor disprove this. Other texts cast doubt on the idea that Athenian citizen women needed to be secluded. In the *Oeconomicus*, when Xenophon mentions a *gunaikonitis* and an *andronitis*, they are not decorated and important parts of the house for maintaining the purity and reputation of his citizen wife or for social dining with other men but a means of controlling the behaviour of male and female slaves to prevent them breeding: 'and I showed her the women's area, separated by a bolted door from the men's' (Xenophon *Oeconomicus* 9.5.1–3). There are also indications in other plays that women were not confined to the house, let alone to quarters in the house. In *Assembly Women* there is no bar on Praxagora leaving the house at night to help at a neighbour's birth (Aristophanes *Assembly Women* 529); the women in this play are able to attend an assembly meeting. A female character in *Women at the Thesmophoria* describes husbands checking other people's homes when their women go missing and finding them sleeping on the couches, presumably after drinking too much (Aristophanes *Women at the Thesmophoria* 795–8). Although this is a comic image, its suggestion that women left the house and socialized with other women must have had some basis in reality for the humour of men chasing and checking up on them to have had an effect. A speech by Demosthenes confirms the idea that women pay visits to each other's houses (55.23–4), and the wife of Euphiletos meets her lover at a funeral, leaves the house to go to the Thesmophoria with his mother and conducts her adulterous affair within her own house (Lysias 1.19–20).

When Euphiletos describes the gender divisions in his house he also reveals that they were not permanent divisions. Following the birth of his child, he moved upstairs, allowing his wife to care for the baby downstairs (Lysias 1.9.6–10.1). His activities are not curtailed by this rearrangement of space: he brings a friend home to dine and they eat upstairs (Lysias 1.22.5–23.5). These passages show flexibility, an ability to change the meaning of space to suit the specific needs of the household: the female areas of the house could simply be all areas that were not occupied by men. Thus, the *gunaikon* only appears when men are in the house and, in particular, when those men are not related to the women of the family (Nevett 1999: 17–19). In these circumstances a *gunaikon* could be created quite easily and on a temporary basis. It could be marked by the use of foliage or textiles, which would warn visitors not to enter. These would simply be removed when it was considered suitable for the women to rejoin the household. In Athens, where houses appear to have been small and urban space restricted, it becomes vitally important that the use of space can be easily manipulated to respond to changing needs. This is an idea that we have already come across in the passage by Aeschines (1.123–4); it can also be seen in a passage from *Protagoras*, when Callias converts a storeroom into a guest room in order to accommodate visiting philosophers (Plato *Protagoras* 315D–E). Individuals managed their domestic space according to their own needs and altered arrangements of space when those needs changed. In fact, the only common feature of each textual appearance of the *gunaikon* is that women can be found there. It is the presence of women rather than architecture that identifies the *gunaikon*. This fits with the linguistic pattern discussed in Chapter 2 where rooms in Athenian houses derive their name and meaning from their use and users. The words *gunaikonitis* and *gunaikon* are used to describe areas in the house that are created to deal with situations where the separation of male and female, whether slaves or husband and wife, is desirable. It is the separation of male and female and respect for their individual needs at specific moments such as childbirth that are controlling the use of domestic space.

If we look more closely at texts concerning female behaviour it is apparent that they present stereotypical images of women rather than accurate depictions of female lives. We are faced with a plethora of fragmented images that show a view consistent with the needs of literary genre and have a decidedly misogynistic trait. The women of tragedy are scary, like Clytemnestra in the *Agamemnon* of Aeschylus, or pitiful, like the helpless women prisoners in Euripides' *Trojan Women*; the Chorus leader in Euripides' *Cyclops* notes that 'there never should have been a race of women' (Euripides *Cyclops* 186–7). The women in the comedies of Aristophanes are often cleverer than the men, an attribute seen as a little unsettling as the women subvert the 'natural' order of the *polis* to take political control in *Assembly Women* and to force the men to end their war by going on a sex strike in *Lysistrata*. This negative view also appears in law and oratory, reinforced by the restrictions placed on women. They were denied citizen rights, they could not make legal contracts, they could not own property and they could not give evidence in court (Isaeus 10.10; Demosthenes 41.8–9). Women should be invisible; neither seen nor publicly named. A further passage from Demosthenes stereotypes women by dividing them into either good wives or sex workers (59.112). Texts thus fit into a pattern of describing female lives by offering a positive or negative representation of female behaviour. The view presented in texts is also supported by imagery, which perpetuates images of women as 'bad' or 'good'. Gravestones and scenes on grave vases often depict images of women in the household, showing them in relation to the men in their life, as wife or mother, or they are secluded and separated from men, indulging in activities that enhance the status of their men, such as admiring their jewellery (see **Fig. 6**). On vases, we see women portrayed either as good wife or whore, which makes it difficult to accept the image as any representation of reality (Lewis 2002); instead we have to see the images on vases and graves as a part of social ideology in the city of Athens. They show us the way that women were perceived rather than how they actually behaved. They are not direct evidence of female behaviour at home.

In the same way, the appearance of the *gunaikon* in texts is an expression of gender ideology, reflecting a desire to show

6 *Gravestone of Hegeso (photo J.E. Morgan)*

that citizen women are pure by controlling their ability to move freely and interact with other members of the community. Texts do not indicate that the *gunaikon* was a specific, permanent or essential architectural feature in a classical Athenian house.

Visiting the men's room in the Athenian house

While women's space was ephemeral and probably more ideal than reality, we can clearly identify the *andron*, the men's room or men's area in the classical Greek house. This is the formal dining room with cement borders present in some but not all of the buildings identified as houses. Here we have a perfect marriage between texts, architecture and ideology—or so it first appears. If we look more closely at the appearances of the *andron* in classical texts, the certainty with which we link texts and architecture can be called into question. Classical texts show that the majority of *androns* were not in the houses of ordinary men and, in most cases, were not even in Athens. Herodotus uses the word on four occasions to describe gender separation in eastern or non-Athenian residences: men in the palace of Croesus live in a suite of rooms, separate from the women (1.34.15–16), and in the tale of the insurrection of Darius we are told that Darius and his co-conspirators broke into the palace at Susa and rushed past the eunuchs to catch the usurper Smerdis, who was in the *andron* (3.77.13–16, 3.78.16–18). Similarly, Polycrates, the tyrant of Samos, is relaxing in a private room or *andron* at his palace (3.121.3–4, 3.123.5–7); Salmoxis builds a public *andron* in Thrace and invites the leading men of the Thracians to dine with him there (4.95).

A similar theme of royal residences and gender divisions can also be seen in the use of the word *andron* in tragic plays. Iphigenia, daughter of Agamemnon, is described as singing for the guests of her father in the *andron* (Aeschylus *Agamemnon* 243–5). Clytemnestra directs visitors to the male area of the palace (Aeschylus *Libation Bearers* 712). A royal *andron* is placed in the residence of Amphitrite, King of Thebes (Euripides *Hercules* 954–5). The idea that palaces had guest sections for important male visitors can also be found in Euripides' *Alcestis* (Euripides *Alcestis* 543). The *andron* in these plays is used as a device to add authority to the poet's portrayal of royal space—its appearance in the text offers a view of the behaviour of royalty, based on knowledge of the behaviour of eastern rulers, for a society that no longer had kings. Public awareness of royal behaviour in the east also contributed to one of the recurring themes of the *Oresteia*; criticizing eastern customs and showing democracy to be right and, ultimately, triumphant. Agamemnon seals his downfall when he behaves like Priam and walks on tapestries (Aeschylus *Agamemnon* 944–9). These initial examples all appear in texts written and performed during the fifth century BC. They show that *androns* were areas used by mythical kings, tyrants and eastern societies for a range of uses, including living, eating, drinking, sleeping and storage. The word *andron* is not being used to describe the presence of an exclusive male dining space located within Athenian classical houses.

Among texts of the late fifth and early fourth centuries BC we do find the word *andron* used in association with houses, yet the link is not a simple one. In *Assembly Women* Praxagora states her intention to turn all of Athens into a house with specific buildings set aside for dining purposes, like the Spartan military mess or *andreion* (Aristophanes *Assembly Women*, 676–7). The Athenian law courts, the primary focal point for disputes between men, will become the place where men eat dinner together, a potent symbol of a community at peace, with its men united. This is not evidence of domestic gender division—Aristophanes is examining solutions to the war through the medium of comedy. Only one Athenian man, Callias, actually owns an *andron*. He gathers a group of men around him for an event hosted in his private space: '. . . and so it seems to me that my preparations would seem more splendid if my *andron* was decorated by men like you whose souls have been purified rather than generals or cavalry commanders or office seekers' (Xenophon *Symposium* 1.4.3–7). This passage refers to a specific space that can be sat in, or stood at the edge of (Xenophon *Symposium* 1.13.1). Yet the invitation to Callias' *andron* deliberately evokes an image of a ruler and his elite band of men or of a king in his royal residence. Given his first-hand knowledge of Persian customs, it is interesting that Xenophon is the only author to use the word *andron* in this way. In Plato's *Symposium*, no reference is made to the room in which the male gathering is held. Xenophon's portrayal of Callias as a man who creates formal and permanent divisions between men and women in his house may be designed to denigrate him—the richest citizen in Athens behaves like a Persian king. Further evidence of Callias' eastern manners can be read in Plato's *Protagoras*, where we are told that Callias' door-keeper is a eunuch. Texts describing the behaviour of the Athenian elite in this period often show them using Persian or eastern symbols to differentiate their activities from other citizens of the *polis*, whether in matters of decoration or dining practices. Callias has taken this behaviour to extremes by creating in his home a space associated with eastern kings.

None of our texts describes the *andron*, except to reveal that it held decorations and weapons, which are not permanent fixtures; the decorations from the *andron* of Polycrates are sent to the Sanctuary of Hera after his death (Herodotus 3.123.5–7). The texts do not indicate that a classical *andron* has a specific or permanent architectural form. A space suitable for male drinking could be created and dismantled as the need arose, a point confirmed by Lysias in 'On the Murder of Eratosthenes', when Euphiletos is able to move his *andronitis* upstairs (1.9–10). In Menander's play *The Door Keeper*, the room where the eating and drinking takes place is called a *triklinos*, a three-couch room (Athenaeus *Deipnosophistae* 71E–F). The room is not being used by a male dining party, but by a family group, including male and female members. Athenian families might need to divide men and women on certain occasions but texts do not indicate that they set aside and marked a specific area of the house to achieve this.

Gender and Athenian houses: the material remains

Investigations of the *andron* and *gunaikon* focus on the belief that words in texts are a terminology proving the existence of spatial separation and showing that specific places were created for men and women in the classical Greek house. We will turn now to the material evidence to see if this belief can be sustained. To begin with, how can we recognize female architecture in the classical Greek house? There are a number of possibilities: first, we could look for evidence of separate living areas for men and women within one building. This would take the form of duplicated spaces: buildings with two courtyards and two sets of reception or living rooms. These are not easy to find in Athenian classical houses. Houses C and D in the Street of the Marble Workers were joined together briefly in the mid-fourth century BC (Young 1951: Fig. 11): the new door led through Room 5 in House C and into the Court in House D. Artefacts found in Room 5 included a wedding vase (*lebes gamikos*), a *pyxis* lid, a drinking cup and a number of stemless drinking cups. The first two artefacts are linked with women, yet the door led into the courtyard of House D, where there was evidence for metal smelting. There is no clear indication that the separation was to create a space specifically for women. It may have been created simply to allow the residents of House C to gain access to the well in House D. There are many divisions in the buildings on the south side of the block at the north foot of the Areopagus. Yet these are completely separate and open directly onto the street. There is no indication that these divisions were related to gender needs.

Secondly, we might look for evidence that buildings have enclosed units of rooms, which attach to the internal spaces of the house but have no external exit. This would suggest that a specific space has been separated from other spaces within the building. An example of this can be seen in evidence from the fifth-century BC architecture of House C: Room 5 offers unique and private access to Room 4. Similarly, access to the rear rooms of the West House on the north slopes of the Areopagus could only be gained by passing through other rooms. The problem with this approach is that even though we can see the division of spaces within a building we have no way of proving exactly who the users were. The rooms at the rear of the West House on the Areopagus contained a stucco-lined tank, which was probably used for commercial or industrial activities. A separated suite is not proof of female separation. Our investigations in the earlier chapters have consistently shown that the private buildings of Athens housed different activities and different users; spatial divisions reveal only that a house could have had more than one group of users. The assumption that such spaces can be related to women is based on the belief that private buildings are exclusively residential—a belief that previous chapters have already cast significant doubt on.

Our third possible means of finding female space is to look for evidence of female artefact assemblages. This is problematic because it relies on the assumption that we can connect women to particular artefacts. In Grave 24 at the Eckterrasse in the Athenian Kerameikos Cemetery, excavators found a body with distinctly female grave goods. There were small boxes or *pyxides* containing cosmetics, mirrors and jewellery, yet bone analysis showed that the body belonged to a young man (Kovacscovics 1990: No. 24). We cannot automatically link artefacts with female users. It may be more likely that women used certain items but it is not definite; even where we find artefacts with female connotations, we cannot link the area to exclusively female use. As we have already seen in Chapter 3, we could be looking at storage places or simply the last place of use for these items. In Athens, the situation is further complicated by the fact that most artefacts are found in wells and not on house floors. As a result, finding female space in Athenian houses is much more difficult. There is no clear evidence for houses with two courtyards; there are no houses with duplicated sets of rooms. We cannot reconstruct the use or meaning when we find internal units of rooms in houses; there are no artefact assemblages to study. The second storey or roof does not survive for us to examine. We cannot see a distinctly female area and, just as the texts suggest a spatial flexibility, we must accept that the material remains also indicate no architecturally defined area was set aside for women in the classical Athenian house.

If we turn to look at male space in the classical Athenian house, while it is true that evidence for *androns* in fifth-century BC Athens exists, these spaces are in the public not domestic sphere. Over the period 437–400 BC, public or religious dining rooms were constructed at four known sites: the Pinakotheke, the Asclepieion, the South Stoa and the Pompeion (Travlos 1971). Rooms were also constructed in the Sanctuary of Artemis at Brauron. A brief study of the rooms in the South Stoa at the Athenian Agora shows that, although they were originally thought to be rooms in a dining block, only one room, Room V, had a cement border. Among the objects found here were the head from a female terracotta figure and a satyr figurine; a marble base designed to hold votive offerings and inscribed with the word 'hero' was found in the south wall of the Stoa between Rooms V and VI (Thompson 1968). Other items found at the South Stoa include terracotta figurines and a *kernos*, a vessel used in religious ritual. This information does not offer us a simple picture of a single use or user, and there is no indication of the gender of the users. The range of artefacts and presence of the altar only show that cult could have played a role in events held here.

Androns begin to be detectable in the remains of Athenian private buildings during the late fourth century BC. They have been identified at Building Z in the Kerameikos, the building on Menander Street, the Central House on the north slopes of the Areopagus and the House of the Greek Mosaic. Other fragments of houses have also been located at excavations throughout the city of Athens (Jones 1975: n. 26). In certain instances they have produced rooms with a square shape and raised borders, but unfortunately no dates can be ascribed to these rooms due to their fragmentary nature. Equally, the excavation reports give little information on what artefacts were found in association with these spaces. We cannot presume knowledge of the users on the basis of architecture or from the name given to these spaces by modern excavators.

It is highly likely that these spaces were not linked to domestic activities but to religion. The earliest examples of these rooms come from sanctuaries, such as the Sanctuary of Demeter and Kore at Corinth. Evidence here seems to indicate that the rooms were used by women (Bookidis et al. 1999), and it seems reasonable to suggest that the rooms were originally designed for use in connection with festivals and cult dining. Inscriptions of the third and fourth centuries BC point to an increase in the numbers of private cult associations at Athens (Leiwo 1997); this period coincides with the emergence of such rooms in urban buildings in Athens. Increasing numbers of small, private cult groups may well have fuelled an expansion in the demand for suitable meeting places. The inscriptions record that some of the groups owned properties, *oikia*, at which they held cult dinners (Hedrick 1990). These *oikia* may be difficult to identify in the material record and it is possible that some of our 'houses' with formal dining rooms are buildings used by cult groups. This likelihood appears to be confirmed by an inscription, which notes: 'And whenever the *orgeones* [cult group] sacrifice to the hero at Boedromion, Diognetos will prepare the *oikia* [building] where the shrine is, and having been opened [he will prepare] the shelter and the cooker and couches and tables to two *triclina*' (Osborne 1988: 287).

While an *oikia* is a built structure, it does not necessarily have to be a large building; it may be a small construction housing an altar or an image or a room in a larger building. This would allow the lessee, Diognetos, to use the land or building around the shrine for his own purposes during the rest of the year. When the cult group wished to dine, Diognetos was required to prepare a dining room and cooking space for them. The inscription does not use the term *andron* to describe the dining space.

The evidence from Athens raises more questions than it answers; in particular it casts doubt on the idea that these rooms are designed specifically for domestic purposes. If they are an essential part of domestic space, why are they not present in every house? We cannot be certain of the users' gender or of the occasion when the room was used: all we can be certain of is that we should not assume that these rooms prove the existence of a house. We cannot point to them as evidence of male space and there is no firm evidence for the creation of exclusively male and female spaces in the classical houses of Athens.

Gender separation at Olynthus

As we have no texts, we have no direct information about the ideology and practice of gender relations in Olynthian society. We can only examine architecture and images of women, which take the form of figurines and scenes on red-figure vases

(Robinson 1933, 1950). While the figurines offer a view of dress and activities such as dancing, they are isolated and not part of any scene with information on the social, political or religious context of the women's actions. It is also the case that we do not know whether the figurines are intended to portray women or female deities. Most red-figure vases show mythological scenes, and where women appear in them it is clear that the image has divine connotations. This restricts our ability to use the images as evidence for female lives. A goddess could step outside the constraints of everyday life; an ordinary woman would not necessarily replicate her behaviour. The scenes that exist showing contemporary women place them in three specific occasions: in the symposium, at worship and in a pre-wedding scene. These scenes may offer an insight into when it was considered acceptable for women to become visible. The women at the symposium are young flute girls, playing to entertain the men; they are not participating in the main event and we are given no indication of their social status. Women are also shown on occasions where their actions have a religious character. They make offerings at altars, they are placed next to cult statues and next to cult artefacts such as incense burners. In pre-wedding scenes, the bride-to-be is shown reclining in an interior space while other women bring her gifts. All women, irrespective of social status, wear clothes that cover them from head to toe. The only exception to this is the bride, who wears a diaphanous robe. She is shown in an interior space, surrounded by other women and dressed seductively for her groom, who will ensure her passage from virgin to wife. In most cases the women also cover their hair by wearing a headscarf or partial veil, a feature that is also present in figurines of women. The practice of veiling is taken to extremes in two relief vases that show women's heads swathed in thick veils covering the whole head, with only the eyes visible (see **Fig. 7**). To summarize, women are only visible in certain situations, they cover themselves from neck to toe and wear headscarves or veils. This suggests a limit on women's visibility in the public arena (Llewellyn-Jones 2003). It is possible that this is evidence of control, which could extend into domestic architecture.

7 *Line drawing of plastic vase from the Villa of Good Fortune, Room (k), Olynthus (from Robinson 1933: n. 406A, Pl. 124)*

If we apply the same search criteria from our Athenian investigation to the buildings of Olynthus, we find the same results. First, there are no examples of the replicated courtyards and associated suites of rooms in the houses. Although some buildings appear to be divided, they have two entrances, meaning that women either lived in complete separation from men, being visited by the men when it suited them, or that women had to come out into the street in order to enter the male portion of the house. Neither of these explanations is satisfactory and so we must assume that these divisions were not the result of gender needs. There are, however, examples of separated units within the house. Most of these are a part of what excavators call the *oecus* or kitchen complex. This consists of a set of two or three rooms, always including a main room with a central hearth and a long room attached to this, called the 'flue' and sometimes including a small third room with a bath (see **Fig. 8**). The link between hearths and cooking is often seen as sufficient reason to identify this as female space, but this idea rests on the erroneous assumption that kitchens are essentially a female domain. While this may have been true in the more recent past, it is wrong to import this assumption to the ancient past. Cooking was a job for slaves, and the gender of slaves was immaterial. To assume that such areas were female erodes the distinction that existed between citizen women and slaves. More persuasively, the hearths of Olynthus contained no evidence of cooking, and the suite itself was not a common feature within buildings at the site. There is no guarantee at Olynthus that the presence of a hearth indicates female space.

Another means of identifying female spaces in the classical Olynthian house could be to locate female artefacts. In practice, this tends to mean looking for concentrations of loom weights. In his assessment of House A viii 7/9, Robinson notes the presence

8 The oecus *unit in Building A2, Olynthus (photo J.E. Morgan)*

of loom weights and suggests that women occupied this area (1946). Similar concentrations of loom weights can be found in the House of Many Colours. Again, we reveal our own 'gender' bias; we assume that women did the weaving at Olynthus. It is equally possible that, as with cooking, slaves performed this task. House A viii 7/9 contained an exceptionally large number of loom weights, which might point to an industrial practice rather than a domestic one. Also present in the same area were incense burners, female masks, storage amphorae and vessels for eating and pouring. This may be a place where slave or free women worked but there is no clear separation in the architecture. The artefacts lie at the end of a long, open porch space, which may have been a storage area. Concentrations of such artefacts show us only that women might have been present, not that they were present in a specific area of the house set aside for their exclusive use. The truth is that we cannot point to any of the areas in the

Olynthian buildings and conclude that they were exclusively female spaces.

While the words *andron* and *gunaikon* come from Athenian textual sources, the structural classification of the *andron*, the men's room, is based on the many rooms with cement borders present in the city of Olynthus. Yet even here, the *andron* is not ubiquitous: we do not find one in every building, which suggests that they were not an essential part of domestic space in this community. The greater number of dining rooms at Olynthus may be the result of a number of different, environmental factors. It could be due to the quantity and quality of evidence: the larger number of urban buildings available for study here may simply have yielded a higher number of these rooms. The better preservation of the buildings at Olynthus might also have made it easier to locate such rooms, while the centuries of rebuilding at Athens may well have eroded evidence of cement borders.

In order to consider the role of these rooms at Olynthus, it is necessary to look at them in more detail. If we begin by looking at the layout and decoration of the rooms, we can see that the most common feature is the raised cement border (see **Fig. 9**). The second most common feature is the coloured paint or stucco on the walls; the colour and border are certainly designed to send a clear message to the entrant about the events that take place here, which could be social, political or religious occasions. The cement borders are clearly set out for users—in a practical sense, they are designed for seating, whether on couches or cushions. Yet the position of the border around the walls of the room can also be read as having a further symbolism; it allows the individuals in the room to view the other participants and, in doing this, it creates and binds a human circle, a group. This is emphasized by the mosaics present in the rooms, whose most common feature is the presence of a circle or encircling motif.

9 Andron in Building A vi 6, Olynthus (photo J.E. Morgan)

The dominance of the circle, symbol of the group, is interesting. The Athenian Tholos, which was used for the *prytaneis*—the executive council—to sleep and dine while on duty, was a round building. The circle plays a significant role in describing the cult group and the family group: the sacrificial group gathers around the altar, the family is defined by those who gather symbolically around the hearth, the circle encloses and protects the participants to the exclusion of those outside the circle. There is nothing exclusively male in these features.

Some mosaics have figured scenes, yet the message contained within the mosaics is not absolutely clear and there are many possible answers. The mosaic floor in Room (a) of the Villa of Good Fortune carries an image of Dionysus, the god of wine (see **Plan 4**, p. 175). This may be a suitable image for a male social gathering, but Dionysus is also a god who is strongly linked to women (Jameson 1993: 61). He is the god who encourages women to break away from the house and dance with him. The followers of Dionysus, the Maenads, are also present in this image, dancing in a circle around the figure of the god. The god is placed at the centre while the Maenads turn out to face the human circle seated on the borders: human and Maenad unite in a circle around the god. The mosaic in the outer chamber faces inwards, towards the Dionysus mosaic, giving a sense that the two rooms are enclosed and separated. This mosaic shows a very masculine image of Achilles arming, but his mother Thetis, donator of the armour, is also present. If we look at the images of women presented by the two rooms, we can see an interesting contrast. In the outer chamber we have an image of the good but over-indulgent mother; in the inner chamber we have an image of destructive mothers. We have the two poles of female maternal behaviour—too doting or not caring at all. It is an image that carries as much meaning for women as for men.

If we take a more contextual approach and look at all aspects of these rooms, their position, decoration and artefacts, we produce interesting insights that emphasize the range of uses to which these rooms could be put. Building A vi 3 has a formal dining room, Room (b), with a mosaic of Bellerophon (see **Fig. 4**, p. 62). It is situated in the northern part of the house. Facing Room (b) is a courtyard paved with a mosaic floor, at the centre of which is a rectangular depression that may have contained an altar. This space is directly opposite the door to Room (b) and could have been visible from the room. The arrangement of space resembles the relationship between altar and temple in sanctuary contexts, perhaps a deliberate parallel. In A xi 9, the room with a cement-border opened onto a court, which took up two-thirds of the available space in the house. The size of the court is exceptional; it would have offered a good space for meetings of larger political or social groups, and the presence of a dining room here may be connected to that. In B v 1, Room (a) offers unique entrance into Room (b), which contains a cement border and an elaborate mosaic, showing a lion bringing down a stag and sphinxes. These two rooms are separated from the rest of the building with their own entrance from Room (a) into the porch area (e) next to the main door of the house. There were twenty-eight coins in the building and few other artefacts. Twenty-one of the coins were spread throughout the northern part of the structure in which the anteroom and *andron* lay, making it a strong possibility that these rooms were available for hire rather than being the exclusive space of a family.

In most cases, the bordered rooms contain no artefacts. Cahill attributes the absence of special sympotic artefacts at Olynthus to the possibility that valuable metal dining sets were taken when the site was abandoned, but it is equally possible that the rooms were simply not used as storage places (2002: 187). The ambiguous nature of the decoration and the absence of artefacts may also reflect the possibility that the room could be adorned for specific and different types of occasions whether attended by male social groups, members of a local cult organization, families or even women alone. Images and equipment could be easily moved into a space or moved around to alter the meaning of the space to suit different occasions. As we have already noted, the cement border area may not have supported permanent couches but cushions or small portable beds, thus allowing a range of events and groups of users to participate in events hosted within the space. The absence of artefacts reflects the multi-functional nature of these space—different users could 'own' and customize the space according to their needs. When we put aside an approach that focuses on similarities and begin to study these spaces in context, it becomes less likely that they are exclusively male space or the *andron* of Athenian texts. Equally, these rooms cannot be used as a sign that the building containing them is a house.

Gender and the 'houses' of Halieis

At Halieis we find similar problems in locating female spaces through architecture alone. Houses D and E have two courtyards but each courtyard is placed in a section that is completely separated by a wall and has its own discrete entrance onto the street. There are suites of rooms present in the buildings, yet these can either be related to the separation of work activities or offer no indication of their use or users. Internal divisions are not present in every building at Halieis. The hearths present at Halieis seem to have been used for cooking, and the large quantities of eating and drinking pottery found in House 7 suggest that the hearth here was used for commercial cooking activities. However, even if women performed the cooking, the room with the hearth, Room (7-16/17), is open rather than closed; there is no seclusion here (see **Plan 7**, p. 176). In House E the hearth is in a small space—too small to operate as living quarters—and opens directly onto the courtyard (see **Plan 10**, p. 178). Women using these areas cannot have been segregated and there is no reason to assume that this was their principal living space. Similarly, there are no great deposits of loom weights through the buildings. The architectural evidence does not indicate that women were separated from men within the buildings of Halieis.

Rooms with cement borders exist in both the public and the urban sphere. They can be found in the sanctuaries of Halieis and in the city buildings. Room (7-9) is part of a two-room unit in the north-west corner of House 7, near to the front door.

The outer room (7-10) gives exclusive access to the inner room (7-9). Room (7-9) has a white plaster floor with a recessed inner area. A channel runs from the central area across the south-east section of the platform and into a small plain-ware jar, which is plastered into the ledge. The jar contained a small black-glazed bowl and a black-glazed stemless drinking cup. This arrangement may have had either a ritual function as a catch-basin for the pouring of libations or a secular function for cleaning the room. We have already mentioned the deposit of pottery found in the street outside this building. The pottery, hearth and presence of the cement-bordered room are similar to the archaeology of the House of Many Colours and suggest that the rooms at Athens, Olynthus and Halieis may have a common function as meeting places, whether available for hire or owned by specific cult or social groups.

There are two other rooms with cement borders at Halieis, one in Area T and another in Area 5 of the city (Jameson 1969: 392; Boyd and Rudolph 1978: 345), but unfortunately neither of the buildings in which they are located have been fully excavated. The room in Area T had a border and also a small base set into the border itself. The excavator suggested that the base was designed to support a cupboard—an interpretation that appears to be inspired by the belief that this was male drinking space. The base would have been equally suitable as a stand for a small altar, a figurine or a brazier. A similar base, inscribed with a reference to a hero was found near the bordered room in the South Stoa at Athens. Another exists in Olynthus in Building A vi 10, Room (a), where a portable altar and hearth were also present. The sanctuary in the Acropolis at Halieis was small, but the Sanctuary of Apollo outside the walls appears to have had dining rooms; there was also a small sanctuary to Demeter to the north of the city. Unlike Olynthus, where no temple or communal dining spaces were found, the presence of such rooms at sanctuaries meant that there was less demand for them in the rest of the settlement and would help to explain why they are not as ubiquitous at Halieis and Athens as at Olynthus.

Observations

Athenian texts reflect ideology rather than practice. This is why the certainty with which we can identify gendered space in texts is not reflected in material remains either at Athens or at non-Athenian sites. There is no clear evidence of a female space in any of our classical Greek houses. It may have existed but its users and use are not permanently encoded in architecture. Given the spatial flexibility indicated in texts, it is highly possible that gender segregation was a temporary state of affairs and achieved through simple, temporary arrangements in the use of space or through the use of textiles. Although we claim that we can identify male space, a deeper study of the rooms with cement borders reveals little to suggest that the users were exclusively male or that the rooms were created in response to male social needs in the domestic context. While men could have used the rooms for sympotic drinking parties, the name *andron* implies an exclusivity that is not borne out by the evidence. These rooms only confirm that the buildings of the classical city could house religious as well as secular and economic activities; they do not indicate that a building is a house—it is by no means certain that they were domestic spaces.

CHAPTER 6

RELIGION AND
THE CLASSICAL HOUSE

In modern 'new' cities, religious attention is focused on buildings in the public sphere. There is often a main building, a church, mosque or temple at the centre of the community, around which the community has grown. There are also smaller local religious buildings woven through the city, each catering to needs of a local urban group. Although the house and household may perform religious acts at home, it is the influence of the doctrinal organization maintaining the public buildings that tends to dominate religious life. This is not necessarily the pattern that we find in a classical city.

In Athens, we can clearly see the temple of their tutelary deity, Athena, set up for city worship. Yet the remains of the temples and shrines that littered the urban landscape are not the property of doctrinal organization but set up by individuals as well as social and familial groups. Evidence from Athenian texts indicates that the house too played an important role in religious life. This is reinforced by archaeological evidence from the city, in which cult inscriptions and altars are set up by family members in the spaces of the city, and hearths and other cult artefacts are found within the houses. In contrast, the religious landscape at Olynthus and Halieis shows a very different picture. At Olynthus, evidence for religious buildings was more noticeable by its absence; at

Halieis, most religious evidence appeared to be outside the city wall. Did these differences extend into the domestic sphere? In our final investigation we will examine evidence for the religious role of the classical house, and discover what our sources can tell us about the role and practice of religion in houses at Athens, Olynthus and Halieis and the religious relationship between house and community.

Religion and the classical Athenian house: a textual perspective

Athenian texts offer us a great deal of information about household religion. The main body of this information is concerned with household gods and household sacrifices. Certain gods are worshipped in the house, and their cult places are woven into the fabric of the building. Hermes and Apollo are both mentioned as guardians of the front door; Hermes took the form of a herm, a pillar with the head of the god. A passage by Thucydides records that: 'In the meantime those herms of stone in the city of Athens—they are the pillars of square construction which according to local custom stand in great numbers both in private and sacred *prothyrons*—nearly all had their faces mutilated on the same night' (Thucydides 6.27.1–2).

Hermes' role was protective; he was the guardian of those who crossed the threshold, the gap between city and household space. The mutilation of the herms by anonymous assailants shocked the Athenian people—it was as if protection had been removed from their houses. Apollo too had a presence at the front door. This connection is referred to explicitly in *Wasps*: 'O Master, King, Neighbour Agyieus of the front door before the gates, accept O Lord new rites we are beginning as for my father' (Aristophanes *Wasps* 869–74). We are not sure what form the presence of Apollo took here. In 'Against Meidias' (Demosthenes 21.51) and *Birds* (Aristophanes *Birds* 1233) references are made to the streets being filled with the savour of sacrificial meat. The word for streets, *agueia*, is the same as the epithet accorded to Apollo in the passage from *Wasps* above. The connection between 'Apollo of the Streets' and sacrifices may indicate that his cult focused on an altar or place at the front door suitable for sacrifice.

Zeus Ktesios was intimately linked to the family and their wealth, and was often presented as the god who guarded the domestic storeroom. Menander inverts the idea of his protective presence for comic effect in his play *Pseudo-Hercules*: 'Now, whenever I see a parasite going into the *gunaikon* and Zeus Ktesios having not kept the storeroom locked but allowing prostitutes to run in . . .' (Menander *Pseudo-Hercules* 519K).

In the speech 'Against Chiron', the family sacrifice to Zeus Ktesios, and a character in the play *Suppliant Maidens* notes that even when goods are stolen from the house, the grace of Zeus Ktesios will look after the family (Isaeus 8.16–17; Aeschylus *Suppliant Maidens* 443–5). Unfortunately, while the texts refer to acts performed for the god, they give little indication whether his cult focused on a specific artefact. Our only information on this comes from a fragmentary passage by the cult historian Anticleides, who notes that a vessel symbolizing the god was set up and adorned in the domestic storeroom (Athenaeus *Deipnosophistae* 473B–C).

We are given more detailed information about the artefacts associated with our last two domestic gods, Zeus Herkeios and Hestia. Zeus Herkeios is worshipped at the courtyard altar in the palace of Priam, which Priam approaches for sanctuary (Euripides *Trojan Women* 16–17), and access to a common altar of Zeus Herkeios is often used as proof of family relationships

(Sophocles *Antigone* 486–7). Hestia is the eponymous goddess of the domestic hearth. She appears most frequently in tragic plays of the classical period where she and the hearth symbolize royal rule. She defined and described the family; they were an exclusive group, permitted to feast at the household hearth. Her persona was so entwined with the household hearth that it is often difficult to know if the use of the word *hestia* referred to the goddess or the sacred fire. In the forensic speech 'On the Murder of Eratosthenes', where the orator Lysias claims that at no point did the adulterer make contact with the *hestia*, it seems clear that the reference is to a domestic fireplace (Lysias 1.27). Contact with the hearth, the place protected by the goddess, ensured that the suppliant was protected by the gods and should not be harmed.

Texts also offer us a view of animal sacrifices performed by household members in the places where they resided. These sacrifices took place on specific occasions such as the festival of Zeus Ktesios, and also on family occasions such as weddings (Isaeus 8.16–17; Menander *Samia* 673–4). Sacrifices also took place when family members wished to give thanks to the gods. The family of Hercules give thanks for his safe return with a sacrifice at their domestic altar (Euripides *Hercules* 922–30). Although this is a tragic play, there is evidence in other texts that domestic sacrifices were not unusual: in Plato's *Republic* two visitors to a house in the Piraeus enter just after a sacrifice has been performed there (328B–C). In *Peace*, Trygaeus sacrifices an animal at home on an altar (Aristophanes *Peace* 942–1126). This passage gives us a picture of the rituals performed prior, during and after the sacrifice, as well as the sacrifice itself. In *Birds* Xanthias and Manodorus are ordered by Peisetaerus to lift up and carry the basket and *chernips*, the vessel containing holy water (Aristophanes *Birds* 850). At line 958 they are told:

'You, taking the *chernips*, go around [the altar] again.' Other authors also refer to sacrifices and sacrificial ritual at home: Menander mentions the action of circling the altar with sacrificial implements prior to making a sacrifice (Menander *Perikeiromene* 997–8), and Xenophon notes that Socrates sacrificed both at home and at common altars (Xenophon *Memorabilia* 1.1.2). The connection between sacrifice and the house is unequivocal—it appears in every genre of literature from classical Athens.

Other references to cult action and cult places in the household are more fragmentary. We are told that the Superstitious Man makes offerings to his domestic herms, oiling and garlanding them (Theophrastus *Characters* 16), and Clytemnestra describes her late-night libations and sacrifices to the Eumenides at her palace hearth (Aeschylus *Eumenides* 106–9). The texts suggest that these acts were performed regularly and, although their value as evidence is diminished by the extreme portraits presented by the ancient authors in both cases, there are sufficient other passages to indicate that regular offerings were a common part of household life. Offerings of incense are made at the time of the full moon in *Wasps* (Aristophanes *Wasps* 96), and in *Electra*, vegetable offerings are made to Apollo at the door of the palace in exchange for the interpretation of a dream (Sophocles *Electra* 637–59).

Texts also reveal that places were set up in the house in order to worship the gods. A character in a passage by Plato asserts: 'For I also have household altars and shrines and ancestral places and all other things of the same type as other Athenians' (Plato *Euthydemus* 302C). In a fragment from the play *Phasma*, a mother is described as meeting her daughter at a hole between the internal rooms of their neighbouring houses, which has been set up as a shrine area (Menander *Phasma* 49–56). The

Superstitious Man will create a shrine in his house if he sees a snake (Theophrastus *Characters* 16.4).

Not all domestic cult places had a visible or permanent construction. Texts also show us that sometimes individuals created ritual space in the house through ritual action. The importance of ritual behaviour and perception in the creation of cult places is reflected in the comment by Hippocrates that, 'We ourselves fix boundaries to the sanctuaries and precincts of the gods, so that nobody may cross them unless he be pure' (Hippocrates *On the Sacred Disease* 358). In descriptions of domestic sacrifice, individuals purify the altar before the event by sprinkling water around it. This marks the area as a 'special' place, suitable for interaction between gods and men, and also protects it. We know from classical texts that the purification was an important religious ritual that applied to all spaces of the city: the Athenian assembly place was purified before meetings began, temples were purified and the Superstitious Man purifies his house on a regular basis (Aristophanes *Acharnians* 44; Euripides *Helen* 865–7; Theophrastus *Characters* 16.7). Purification cleansed and marked a symbolic boundary, invisibly protecting those within it. In purifying the house the family separated their private area from the city, they marked the walls and symbolically defined and protected their space.

The vital importance of human action in creating a cult space can be read in a passage by Menander. Here an individual who believes he is in love with a ghost is purified in the hope of finding a cure:

> What do I advise? I say this. If this had been a real problem, Pheidias, you would have had to seek a real remedy for this. But yet you have not, so find a fake medicine for your fake illness and believe that it helps you. Let the women in a circle wipe all around you and

burn incense around you. Sprinkle around water from three springs, throwing on salt, lentils ... (Menander *Phasma* 24–31)

Pheidias will sit at the centre; he is the focal point of the action and at the centre of both ritual occasion and ritual space. The ritual space will be created by the women, who surround Pheidias and wipe around him, purifying that area and creating a division between Pheidias' immediate space and the room around him. They also burn a scented substance, which changes the atmosphere within the room and binds together those taking part in the event, defining and identifying them as an exclusive group. Through sight, sound and smell, the meaning given to the space is altered to allow the participants to believe that they and Pheidias are in a space apart. We are not told where the rite will take place; we only know that it will be within the house. The precise location is irrelevant— the rooms in which these acts take place is not important. The ritual space is temporary, its meaning is given by acts and individuals not architecture.

Religion and the classical Athenian house: a material perspective

Despite the fact that the texts make an unequivocal link between cult action, cult artefacts and houses, it can be called into question by the simple observation that few religious artefacts have ever been found in the urban buildings at Athens. We should expect difficulties in finding material evidence of cult behaviour—rituals such as the 'curing' of Pheidias are unlikely to leave a trace in the archaeological record—but the evidence for cult artefacts and places is equally scarce. To date, no evidence has been found for a central altar in Athenian urban buildings, whether in fragments of its structure or in the survival of footings for its placement. There are no stone herms or altars at doors or signs that they were ever placed there. Out of all the urban buildings excavated in Athens, only one had a formal hearth. This was located in a side room in the West House on the north-east slopes of the Areopagus (see **Plan 1**, p. 173). The absence of cult artefacts could be attributed to the clearing of such buildings over time and to the reuse of large stone blocks from hearths and altars. Yet, as we have already noted, we cannot identify Athenian houses clearly, let alone assess which room was a storeroom or which artefact in a storeroom can be linked to Zeus Ktesios.

The discrepancy between our textual and material sources can, in part, be explained by our own expectations. When we think of the objects used in classical Greek cult, we automatically think of artefacts used in the public sphere. The altars, hearths and statues of public cult are large and made of permanent materials such as stone. They are monumental and visible. When we do not find correlates in the private sphere, we assume either that they were not needed, or that there is a flaw in the ability of our sources to show us the correlation. Yet the needs of domestic cult were not the same as those of the public cult. Size and permanence were not as important. If we consider the texts more closely, it becomes apparent that in many cases small or degradable artefacts would have sufficed for domestic worshippers. Although texts clearly link Hermes to the house, they do not confirm either that the artefact connected with him always took the form of a herm, or that it was made of stone. A small wooden figure or representation of the god Hermes could have been carved into the frames of Athenian doors. This type of representation of Hermes can still be seen today—although admittedly from a slightly later period than this study—in the small carving of a herm set into the stone frame of a door at the Stoa of Attalos (Harrison 1965: 141). Evidence shows that herms in the Agora were sometimes carved onto loose bits of stone. There are body parts from miniature herms in the fill among the debris in the Street of the Marble Workers.

These ideas offer more potential to explain the discrepancies between material and textual evidence. If we accept the evidence so far that the 'houses' of Athens were often no more than a few rooms in a larger building, then the discovery of small herms and our failure to find large square stone ones at the main door makes more sense. In a building with many residents, there may be many main doors, and they may open onto the court rather than the street; miniature herms would use less space and have the same religious effect. A similar logic can be applied to the altar of Apollo. His symbol, the bay tree or a bunch of bay leaves, may well have been sufficient to obtain the protection of the god at the front door. Indeed, a bay tree, symbol of Apollo, stands next to the front door in *Wasps* (Aristophanes *Thesmophoria* 489). A fragment by Aristophanes illustrates that protection could be obtained by using temporary materials; he reveals that a head of squill might be buried at the door to protect those within (fr. 255). Textual descriptions of the domestic sacrifice to Zeus Ktesios offer no indication that a large, monumental or specific artefact symbolized the god at this sacrifice or in the storeroom. It may be that something simple, such as a small cup, was reserved for the god to receive his portion at the sacrifices or offerings in his honour.

The same logic may also help to explain the absence of hearths in Athenian houses. We assume that the domestic hearth in texts was permanent and monumental, looking like the central hearth of temples. It is interesting that in each example where cult is being performed or where the hearth is a symbol of the family, the word *hestia* is used to describe the sacred fire. The ordinary needs of a family—the preparation of food and heating or lighting—are not associated with the *hestia*; the word is used for family cult acts and ideological use. In instances where more ordinary household acts are taking place, the term used for the fire is *eschara*, a word that appears in classical literature most frequently in the context of a hearth used for cooking. However, the *eschara* is not always a fixed feature: many references suggest that it was portable (Aristophanes *Acharnians* 887–8). Bread ovens are portable, as are the *escharas* or braziers found in domestic sites at the Athenian Agora. They would not leave much of a deposit on the ground or permit the site of cooking to be discovered in the archaeological remains. These descriptions suggest that it is not the object itself that is relevant but the behaviour and perceptions of the participants. Texts indicate that the roles of domestic rooms could be altered as the needs of the domestic users changed. In the same way, the roles of artefacts might also alter, allowing them to change from domestic to sacred items when needed for rites. With regard to the hearth, any fire would suffice as long as the participants believed it was sacred.

Domestic spaces needed to be multi-functional; it is likely that the act of reserving a whole space for cult acts could only be achieved by the really wealthy. In the crowded city, dwelling space needed to be able to change its meaning as the needs of the users demanded. In such circumstances, ritual action and smaller artefacts would be more relevant in domestic cult. If we accept that monumentality and permanence were not vital parts of domestic cult, it makes it easier to understand Plato's annoyance at the ease and frequency with which householders set up domestic cult places: '... and they set up both *hiera* [shrines] and altars in private houses, thinking by stealth to make the gods gracious by both sacrifices and prayers' (Plato *Laws* 910B).

Ritual action and perception become more important than the development of permanent places. Spaces are marked by purification and behaviour. Artefacts do not have to be large or monumental. When Trygaeus wants to use an altar for his domestic sacrifice, he mentions that he will fetch it (Aristophanes *Peace* 942). This indicates not only that the altar is small enough for a man to carry, but also that the altar is not permanently set up.

Religion and the house in Olynthus

The juxtaposition of Athenian and Olynthian evidence is common in the sphere of domestic cult; scholars have little hesitation in marrying Athenian texts to Olynthian material evidence. While there are certainly many examples of altars, hearths and figurines in the Olynthian buildings, the investigations in our previous chapters have cast doubt on the view that Olynthian buildings were exclusively domestic or the setting for only one family group. The picture offered to us by the material evidence is one of many uses and users. Can we be sure that the cult material can be directly related to family or individual needs?

There are three types of evidence for altars in the private buildings at Olynthus, large fixed altars, miniature altars and altar bases. Large, built and permanently fixed altars can be found in only three buildings, the House of Many Colours, A10 and in A viii 8. The altar in the court of the House of Many Colours, Room (i), consists of several pieces of a limestone canopy found in the south edge of a space $1.20m^2$ lying between the doors to Rooms (h) and (k) in the west end of the court (see **Plan 6**, p. 176). House A viii 8 has a large, rectangular altar made of rubble and covered with white stucco and stucco mouldings, built into the north-west corner, near the entrance to Room (a). The altar in House A10 is free standing; it is set into the west of a portion of the cobble pavement in the court, to the east of Room (i) and has an upright body of stone slabs with decoration. The use of stone slabs indicates that the interior of the altar may have been hollow.

All three altars are in the open areas of the house—the courtyard and porch area—and are similar in size and style; they are placed at the sides of spaces. The altar in A viii 8 is in the corner of a porch area while the other two altars are placed to the west of courts. The buildings that contain them have an interesting archaeology. In the House of Many Colours we have evidence for the large-scale cooking of food and a dining room. As we have already noted, these two features may indicate a commercial enterprise; it is equally possible that they are connected to religious behaviour, to the practice of sacrifice and cult dining. The altar in A10 is also placed close to a formal dining room, and the same connection between altar and formal dining room can be seen in other buildings such as in A vi 3 and the House of the Comedian. In A viii 8 we do not have a dining space but there is an unusual entrance that mirrors the appearance of a temple. The entrance is long and its sides are faced with columns. There are two other altars in the building and a complex at the front that may have been a commercial bakery. The altars are large and visible. Their size, the connection with dining rooms in the case of House of Many Colours and A10, the unusual architecture and quantity of altars in A viii 8 and the similarity between the spatial arrangements of these buildings and temples suggests that these were communal rather than domestic sites. Their location within the building suggests that the altars could be owned and shared by the groups using the building since the open areas afforded access to all users.

In some cases, the evidence for an altar consists of a space or base marked into the ground for its placement. The gaps in A vi 3 and the House of the Comedian are situated at the centre of mosaics in the open court. A number of areas have square or rectangular bases made of dressed stone or limestone, or from small rough stones packed tightly together. The base in the House of the Tiled Prothyon is made of small stones and is positioned at the centre of a cobbled court. The bases have various alignments and are placed at different locations. In each case, the link between space and altar is unproven, as no remains of any altars are present. It is possible that these bases had other functions, for example, as a base for a statue or for a brazier.

. The buildings at Olynthus also contained many miniature altars; these had an average height of 23.4cm, width of 17.1cm and depth of 15.8cm. They offer us a good deal of information about their use. Although small, the altars are functional as much as decorative. Some of the altars had burnt areas at the top, while others had shallow depressions that may have been designed to hold pots or liquid offerings. Their size and portability meant that they could be moved to any location. Some of the miniature altars had flat undecorated backs, which contrasts with the moulding on their other sides and indicates that they were to be placed against a wall. Two such altars are present in the Villa of the Bronzes, Room (e). However, it is clear that not all of the altars were intended for use at the locations where they were found: House A5 and House A10 appear to have been occupied by stonemasons; there were nine portable altars in A5 and the three in the court of A10, all of which were unfinished. The altars are most often situated in the porch areas of the buildings and may be in storage places rather than marking cult spots.

Cahill notes that the miniature altars are often found in pairs (2002: 252, n. 75). There are pairs in A viii 8, Room (a), the Villa of the Bronzes, Room (e), the House of Many Colours, Room (e) and the House of the Tiled Prothyron, Room (a). While this may suggest that the altars were deliberately made and sold in pairs, not all of the altars listed by Cahill are exact matches. In House A viii 8, one altar is a circular column while the other is square, with a cockerel painted in relief. The purpose of keeping pairs of altars may be related to a number of cult or practical considerations: the pairs of altars may represent the two sides of the family, maternal and paternal, remembered at rites in the buildings, or they may be designed for the worship of paired deities, such as the Dioscouroi or Artemis and Apollo. The need to possess a pair of miniature altars might also relate to their function. It could have been considered important by some users to separate their sacrifices: liquids or vegetable and food offerings on one altar and animal sacrifice (blood) at another. Robinson suggests that the red clay miniature altar from A viii 8, Room (e) had raised moulding around its base to catch liquid poured into the depression on top (1946: 45). However, the use of two miniature altars may simply have been an accepted practice in Olynthian households—a regional feature of worship.

The presence of the miniature altars does not necessarily reflect domestic activity or indicate a domestic space. Most of the rooms with miniature altars are unusual and do not appear to have a domestic use. There are four altars in the House of the Tiled Prothyron, Room (a). This building also contained a central altar space in its courtyard and a separated suite of rooms, which contained miniature pottery and a lead dish filled with ashes, which Cahill suggests may have served as a hearth (2002: 146). The suite of rooms appears to have had a ritual purpose, and there is little evidence of residence in the building. In A vi 10, Room (a) the miniature altar was found with a large, fixed hearth. Although it is possible that some altars were used for domestic purposes, their presence in buildings with apparently communal spaces and with monumental artefacts or those that mimic communal cult artefacts suggests that they were not exclusively domestic.

The hearths at Olynthus range in appearance from the marble blocks used to define the perimeter of the hearth in the house of the Comedian, Room (e), to the rough stone blocks used to mark the hearth in A vi 2. They consist of a rectangular or square area of roughly similar size, marked by a border of stone blocks with an inner area holding ashes but no bones (see **Fig. 10**). On the sides of the stone surround evidence of burning shows that fire took place *in situ*. These hearths are also very similar in their location and placement. All are positioned in rooms that adjoin the front or back wall of houses; all are positioned at the centre of that room. The similarities suggest that they may have played a similar role in the house or been constructed for a similar purpose; we will therefore turn to the artefacts present in the rooms to help us decipher what that role was. The first role that we can rule out is cooking: the only clear evidence for cooking in these rooms is the spit and supports found in the House of the Comedian, Room (e). No animal bones are reported as being present in the rooms or the hearths. Cooking ware is similarly poorly represented and the majority of domestic ware appears to be associated with eating rather than cooking. The pottery present would seem to indicate that eating took place here but cooking may have been done elsewhere in the house.

Cahill suggests that, rather than being cooking places, we should see the Olynthian hearths as a means of warming or lighting the house. He notes that the hearth and flues could be used together to generate internal heat and light in the winter months, to enable household chores to continue (2002: 193). This is a practical solution but it does not explain why the hearth is not a feature in every building; Cahill assumes that the hearths are domestic yet they are situated in a suite of rooms, the *oecus*,

10 Hearth from Building A vi 6, Olynthus (photo J.E. Morgan)

that is capable of being closed off and used by a non-residential group (see **Fig. 8**, p. 135). The rooms may have been dining spaces. The square, monumental hearths and their locations bear certain similarities to the shape and central position of hearths in sanctuary buildings. The hearth rooms in sanctuaries have clear evidence of use as a cult dining room (Bergquist 1990). The presence of the bath echoes the arrangement and features of the dining suites in the Sanctuary of Demeter and Kore in Corinth, strengthening the idea that these rooms could have been used by members of the wider community rather than being exclusively domestic. The rooms may also have been bathing complexes. The hearth could have been used to heat water, which was carried into the smaller room that housed a bath, which is often found in these room units.

We see these hearths as religious structures because of our belief that they are the physical manifestation of the hearth in Athenian texts. There is no guarantee that Athenian authors were thinking of this kind of artefact when they wrote. The presence of monumental hearths in the buildings at Olynthus and their absence in the private buildings at Athens suggests that there may have been differences in the way that hearths were used or understood at the two sites.

There are many figurines spread through the Olynthian buildings but it is difficult to connect the figurines to domestic cult. We do not find them serving as a focal point for offerings; we do not know whom they are designed to represent. As discrete figures they can tell us little about cult acts in the buildings. However when we look at them in context, the information they offer is interesting. The assemblage in the House of the Comedian, Room (j) included a large number of *protomes*, masks with religious links that were designed for hanging, with other figurines and vessels for eating and drinking. The artefacts were found together along the south wall of the room and had been displayed together at this location. The room was highly decorated with painted walls, a cement border and a central mosaic. The door faced onto a courtyard, looking directly at an altar. The figurines may have identified the space as religious and played a role in ritual occasions held here.

Our study thus far indicates that in the absence of a large central temple at Olynthus, smaller spaces and areas within the urban buildings may have served the needs of cult. As the community at Olynthus was created by the *synoikism* of local villages, it seems likely that they brought with them the traditional religious practices of their communities and ancestors. In such circumstances, the appointment of a single tutelary deity would be virtually impossible. A far more practical solution would be to allow people the freedom to continue their religious practices. The impact of this on the city landscape would be the creation of a community with no large central temple but a range of other shrines, altars and areas of worship, such as we find at Olynthus. The buildings on the North Hill were also created with a degree of urgency; it appears that the framework of the grid plan was set out and the use of space within it was then established by the purchasers or lessees. If religious places in Olynthus were created by groups, families and individuals, this would help to explain the integration of religious spaces into the urban buildings at the site, and the absence of shrines, altars and statues in the streets of the city. On the occasions where we find clearly identifiable religious places, it is more likely that we are looking at communal rather than domestic areas. Religious evidence is not necessarily proof that a building is a house.

Religion and the house in Halieis

There are no domestic altars in Halieis; no discernible evidence for household altars was recovered during the course of the excavation. Neither did the excavation reveal any sites where an altar may have stood. This deficiency may be a consequence of the smaller size of the sample, yet even expanding the study across all of the areas of domestic excavation at Halieis fails to elicit any certain evidence for domestic altars or for their locations. A building in Area T had a base set into the cement border of a room (Jameson 1969: 392), which may have had a religious function, although there is insufficient evidence to be sure. The excavators at Halieis found small shrine areas set into the streets and into the city wall. Altars appear to be artefacts associated with the communal rather than the urban sphere or they may have been small and removed when the site was abandoned.

In House E, Room (6-24) two blocks of limestone with traces of stucco on their upper surfaces were positioned end-to-end within the floor and were level with the latest floor of the house (see **Plan 10**, p. 178). The blocks were placed midway along the dividing wall with Room (6-25). Immediately to the west of the blocks was a black-glazed drinking cup, a *bolsal*, while one miniature *skyphos* was buried between the two blocks and one between the blocks and the wall, apparently placed there when the blocks were laid or buried. The blocks had an inscription, referring to Zeus and ancestral heroes, which Jameson suggests is a reference to family cult (2001: 201). Room (6-24) is on the east side of the house, positioned between the back room of the two-room suite and Room (6-25). It has no evidence of decoration and opened onto the court, but its location to the right of the court prevented those entering the house from seeing into the room. It also appears to have been screened from view by the presence of a stairwell between the two rooms.

The blocks may be a ritual burial given to a sacred inscription or a manifestation of household ancestral cult. Yet it is interesting that this is the only example we have of this type of deposit at Halieis. It is certainly not a common domestic practice. The upper surfaces of the blocks were at floor level and were covered with stucco, clearly marking out the space where they lay. Jameson suggests that this position was not their original location, as the inscriptions would not have been visible (2001: 197), but this presumes that the inscription was intended for reading. The blocks may well have been created specifically for the purpose of setting up a cult. The burial of the blocks and the inscription removed the inscription from view, making it a private and exclusive gesture for the deities concerned. The presence of miniature *skyphoi*, buried with the inscription, suggests that liquid offerings or libations were made here when the blocks were buried.

There are two hearths present in the five houses. In House 7 the hearth is situated at the end of a spur wall and between two rooms (7-16 and 7-17). It consists of a 25cm^2 ash deposit with two upright slabs that form part of its confining perimeter surviving *in situ* and is located at the edges of a space opening onto the courtyard (see **Plan 7**, p. 176). We have already noted the potential role of this hearth as a cooking hearth. The second hearth is in House D, Room (6-30) and measures approximately 65cm x 75cm and is open to its south-east side with a perimeter constructed of mud brick. It is in a small internal room and almost fills the available area (see **Plan 10**, p. 178). It is clearly the central feature of the room but, as the room is very small, it bears no resemblance to the spatial arrangements of the hearth rooms at Olynthus. The hearth is packed with ceramic debris that does not reflect its use during its lifetime but rather its role on the abandonment of the house.

Observations

In Athens we have many texts but little material evidence. At Olynthus there is evidence for cult, but it appears to be communal rather than domestic. At Halieis we have a mix of communal cult places and also evidence in the buildings for smaller-scale cult acts. The variation in evidence at our sites may reflect the different social and political ideologies within our communities. At Athens, the democratic ethos meant that religious actions were performed for the benefit of all and were a communal matter, performed in the public places of the city. We can see this in a passage by Theophrastus where the character Petty Ambition nails a skull to his front door to show everyone that he has sacrificed in style (Theophrastus *Characters* 21.7). In many cases where larger animals were sacrificed, the offering, butchering and cooking of the animal was dealt with by a professional specialist, the *mageiros*; it is possible that the sacrifice took part on public altars, with the consumption being reserved for the house (Wilkins 2000: 369–414). Large cult areas were neither necessary nor feasible within private urban buildings. Athens encouraged its citizens to participate in public religious life; even private rituals such as marriage included a public element. At Olynthus there is no evidence of monumental public religious sites. Although religious acts may have been performed at a distant site, it is possible that religion was seen as a necessary act but not one performed in full view of the community—religious actions were enclosed rather than open. Thus, communal religion was incorporated into urban buildings. At Halieis, the small size of the settlement meant that the area within the walls was mostly reserved for habitation. The shrines that exist are small; apart from the acropolis, the major temples are outside the city. There is therefore little in the private buildings to show religious behaviour. The evidence that does exist shows that domestic cult was highly personal and small in scale. The burying of an inscription in House E appears to be the result of a very individual decision, and the ritual was certainly not repeated in any other building in the city. Miniature shapes, replicas of those found at sanctuaries, litter the buildings and may have played a part in private cult acts at Halieis.

For the most part, our investigation has turned up evidence of communal behaviour. If it is true that the house played a vital role in the religious life of a classical city, why can we not see this? Our investigation of Athenian texts suggested that ritual action was more important than permanent artefacts within the household; small, temporary artefacts could be imbued with ritual meaning if the correct rituals were performed. It is interesting that one factor common to the material evidence from the urban buildings at each of our sites is that the vast majority of 'religious' artefacts are small. Altars, where found, are of the small, portable, variety, figurines are generally between 10 and 20cm in height, and items such as incense burners, miniatures and amulets are all small in scale. While the smaller size of private artefacts may be a consequence of the practical needs of the household, the size may also be a significant factor in cult rites: size can be used to distance the participant from the real world, to create a separate world. Hippocrates (*On the Sacred Disease* 358) mentions the importance of creating boundaries between the spaces of men and the spaces of gods, but these boundaries can be constructed by behaviour and artefacts. Dimensionality can alter the participant's view of his setting and allow the belief that a 'special' place has been created (Bailey 2005: 34). Images on vases show gods as taller than men. This is not necessarily a statement about perceived height but a way of rationalizing the meeting of gods and men and their interaction by creating a 'special' place. In the act of holding or placing miniature items the participant separates himself and his immediate area from the 'real' world. Just as ritual action can separate a space for interaction with the supernatural, so the act of holding and using miniatures can allow the participant to believe that they are apart from the rules of the normal world. The use of small artefacts by ritual participants may well have articulated a difference between domestic space and ritual space. Miniature artefacts could have helped to create an area suitable for the interaction of man and god in the domestic context. The portable nature of domestic artefacts and their use in rites within the house could change the way in which specific spaces were viewed, thus making domestic spaces into ritual spaces.

The religious evidence from Athens, Olynthus and Halieis is very varied and shows that the cities had different attitudes to the religious relationship between house and city. No single behavioural model fits all cases. We know that the house played a vital role in the religious life of the classical Greek city, we can see religious evidence in urban buildings, but the clearest evidence of religious practices is not necessarily evidence of domesticity.

Final Observations
and Thoughts

This book has examined the classical Greek house from a contextual perspective. It has looked at the material and textual evidence in its unique urban setting, avoiding the assumption that all places of residence will look the same or be used in the same way. It has considered the roles played by the house in a community and the impact of communal political, social, economic, religious and gender ideologies and behaviour on the shape and use of the house itself. The results have been surprising.

While in modern western cities the house carries a singular meaning as the private space of a family, and its architecture can be easily identified, this is not the case in the cities of classical Greece. It is certainly possible to identify domestic behaviour and to locate that behaviour in texts and even in vase images. Yet when characters speak about the house, they give us no indication of its appearance or its size. Texts do not give us an accurate description of the size, layout or decoration of houses. As a result, when we come to identify houses in the material record, we are swayed by our own cultural bias, and the fact that most buildings have only one front door, into believing that they are a unified building, exclusively residential and the location of one family. We ignore the possibility that one building could have housed many families. We also ignore the evidence that, while one portion of a building was residential, another portion might have a different use; activities such as industry, trade and even entertainment could have taken place in the same building. If we find evidence for these activities, then the presence of a single front door in one private building is not enough reason to describe the building as a house.

We also assume that, because we can identify certain features in private buildings, this means that they are houses. When we find altars and hearths, we equate these with domestic worship. When we find an *andron*, we think we are looking at a domestic space. We impose our own, mistaken readings of classical Athenian texts onto the material evidence without thought for geographical and contextual differences between cities, without consideration of the complexities of texts and the dangers inherent in turning terms from ancient texts into modern architectural labels. We create a monstrous hybrid of ancient and modern ideas that reflects our own culturally based understanding of domesticity and strangles the uniqueness of the material evidence. We seek to find houses that we can recognize among the remains of the classical city. We do not see that the past is a very different place.

Houses are difficult to identify and explain. Our investigations have cast doubt on the way that we approach the evidence, on the evidence itself and on the degree to which we should use the term 'house' to describe private buildings in classical Greek cities. Spatial meaning is neither fixed nor permanent. A room is just a built space; a house is just a building. Meaning is added by the presence of individuals and artefacts and by their behaviour at a specific time. As a result, rooms can change their meaning to suit the needs of the household. It is also possible that one room can hold several meanings: the different areas within a room can be marked by the use of screens, textiles or artefacts; one building can be used by several different social groups who mark their space using methods that archaeology cannot recover. This idea of flexibility fits better with the lack of clear evidence for function-specific domestic spaces and with material evidence for multiple users and for the presence of many 'houses' within a single building.

A study of the varied roles played by 'houses' can offer us insights into the relationship between house and city; it shows their mutual dependence, ability to influence each other's physical structure and use to reflect and reinforce practical and symbolic patterns of behaviour. A search for the houses of Athens reveals a clear distinction between public and private spaces. Public buildings are large and visible; houses are harder to identify. This reflects the democratic politics of the city where public spaces are of vital importance to the maintenance of the constitution. Private buildings are less important: they are built of less durable materials and have little decoration or elaboration, they are functional. The number of private buildings in the city reflects the size of the community. In Athens, the buildings needed to host a large citizen body and also a large non-Athenian community who could not own land. The divisibility of buildings provided a quick solution to this, so that one building could house many families. The demand for space also affected the urban economy. The private buildings of Athens supported many economic activities. Some of these were of a large-scale and intrusive nature, in which case the activities were integrated into single buildings alongside commercial and residential quarters. Evidence for religious behaviour is slight: there is little in the private buildings and copious quantities in the public sphere, which suggests that, like politics, religion is an act practised for the benefit of the community. Household religion is small, temporary in nature and difficult to locate.

In contrast, our search for 'houses' at Olynthus found significant differences in the organization and use of both domestic and urban space. There are no large, visible public buildings, nor are there any large religious buildings. Evidence for public and religious activities is spread through the 'houses' in the city. Some buildings mimicked the structure of temples and shrines, others had monumental and expensive decoration, but this was contained within the building rather than being made visible to the community at large, as it was in Athens. The buildings also hosted a range of economic activities that appear to have been set into separated spaces within the buildings; within these same buildings, we can identify areas where residence occurred. This confirms that the label 'house' is wildly inappropriate at Olynthus. The full range of public and private activities practised by classical cities can be found in single Olynthian buildings. Studying the roles played by 'houses' here suggests that Olynthus had a different political constitution to Athens and a different cultural mind-set. Large-scale public meeting places are not required. Public display is not acceptable; religious, social and possibly administrative behaviours are internalized and carried out inside the buildings at the site. Buildings can have many uses and users. The Olynthian house need not have been a whole discrete building but only a section within a private building.

At Halieis, we can identify public and private buildings. The majority of public buildings are placed outside the city. These may have been used by other communities as well as Halieis, or their location may reflect the political instability faced by Halieis. The walls are the most visible public feature, indicating that providing a protection for citizens in times of danger was of paramount importance. Although the buildings are subdivided and have evidence for economic activities alongside residential evidence, this evidence is on a small scale and agricultural. The economic evidence is integrated into the layout of the building rather than separated or isolated. The buildings indicate a need for self-sufficiency in the provision of essentials such as food. This is perhaps not surprising given the insecurity of the region. It is more likely that the buildings operated as individual houses rather than *synoikia*.

If we study houses as individual buildings, we limit our view. At the Vari House, we can only classify the architecture and offer simple explanations for room use. We need to consider houses in their urban context if we are to learn more about the roles that they played in their communities and the effect of the community on the presentation and use of the 'house'. The urban layout and urban buildings at Athens, Olynthus and Halieis share some similarities but also display significant differences. Their differences reveal unique political, social, economic, gender and religious ideologies and practices; they offer us an insight into urban life, domestic life and, perhaps most importantly, into life in communities outside Athens. Above all else, a contextual study of domesticity in the classical city suggests that we cannot and should not view classical houses as a mere reflection of our own domestic practices.

HOUSE PLANS

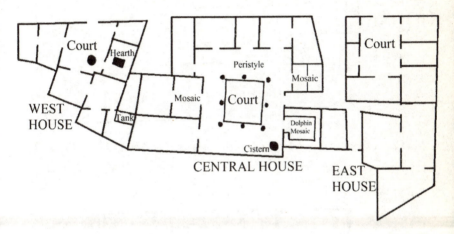

1 *Plan of houses on the north-east slopes of the Areopagus (based on Shear 1973: Fig. 4)*

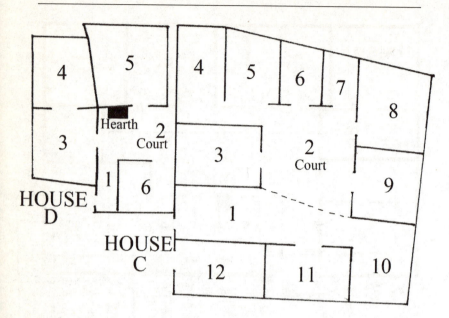

2 Plan of House C and House D, Athens (based on Young 1951: Fig. 11)

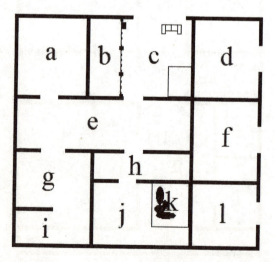

3 Building A iv 9, Olynthus (Robinson 1946: Pl. 98)

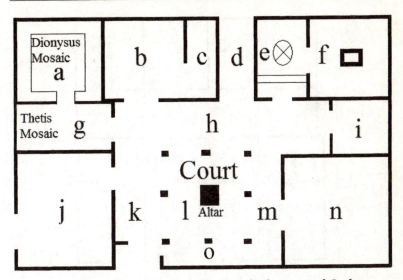

4 *The Villa of Good Fortune, Olynthus (Robinson and Graham 1938: Pl. 84)*

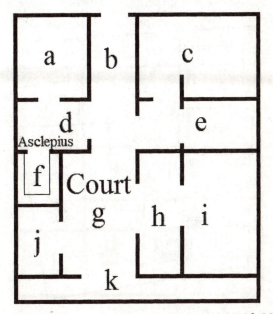

5 *Building B vi 7, Olynthus (Robinson 1946: Pl. 98)*

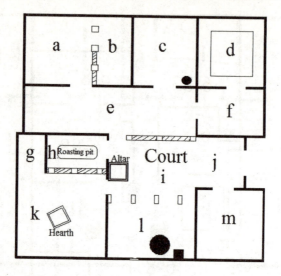

6 *House of Many Colours, Olynthus (based on Robinson 1946: Pl. 158)*

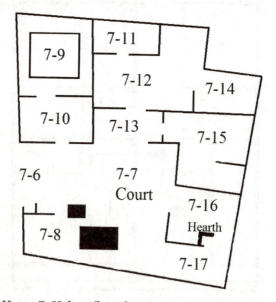

7 *House 7, Halieis (based on Boyd and Rudolph: Fig. 3)*

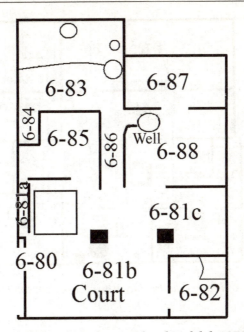

8 *House A, Halieis (based on Boyd and Rudolph 1978: Fig. 3)*

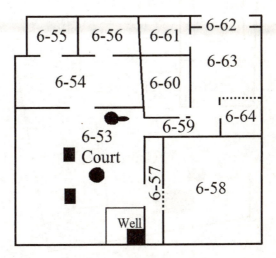

9 *House C, Halieis (based on Boyd and Rudolph 1978: Fig. 3)*

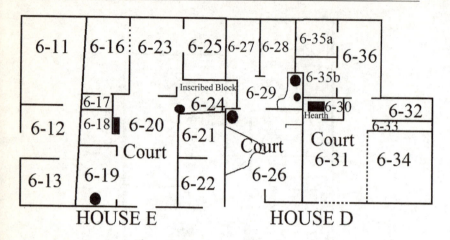

10 *Houses D and E, Halieis (based on Boyd and Rudolph 1978: Fig. 3)*

SUGGESTIONS FOR
FURTHER READING

Further details about the buildings mentioned in this volume can be read in the excavation reports of the various sites.

A report on the Vari House can be read in Jones, Graham and Sackett (1973).

For Athens, individual reports on the buildings can be read in the journal *Hesperia*. Houses C and D can be found in Young (1951), the block of buildings on the north foot of the Areopagus are in Thompson (1959) and the buildings on the north-east slopes of the Areopagus are in Shear (1973). A summary of the buildings in the Agora can be found in Thompson and Wycherley (1972) and Camp (2001). General details about Athenian houses can be found in Graham (1966) and Jones (1975).

For the buildings at Olynthus, there are a large number of excavation volumes that focus on the different types of architecture and artefacts. The 'domestic' buildings are dealt with in Robertson and Graham (1938) and Robertson (1946). All other volumes can be found in the bibliography under 'Robinson'. A more recent examination of evidence from the site can be found in Cahill (2002).

The buildings at Halieis are described by McAllister (2005) and Ault (2005), and in articles by Jameson (1969) and Boyd and Rudolph (1978).

Sources

Several books deal with the use of ancient sources. Crawford (1983) offers a series of essays that deal with each type of source separately. More specific treatments of individual sources can be found in Bagnall (1995), Beard and Henderson (2001), Howgego (1995), Lewis (2002), Renfrew and Bahn (1991) and Shanks (1995).

Greek and English versions of all the ancient texts referred to in this book can be found in the volumes of the Loeb Classical Library Series and also on the website www.perseus.tufts.edu. For extra information on the texts, the Aris and Phillips Classical Texts Series offers an excellent range of commentaries.

Houses

There are a number of volumes devoted to examining aspects of the classical Greek house. Nevett (1999) looks at the relationship between structure and social practice. Jameson (1990) looks at the relationship between house and settlement. In an edited volume Allison (1999) and others consider the relationship between rooms and their artefact assemblages, while Ault and Nevett's (2005) edited volume explores material evidence from a range of domestic sites. More general studies such as Whitley (2001) and Travlos (1971) include the evidence for houses at various sites.

Household and Community

Detailed studies of the development of cities in ancient Greece have been made by Hoepfner and Schwandner (1986), Owens (1991), Tomlinson (1992) and Wycherley (1962). Collections of essays on the subject have can be found in Murray and Price (1990) and Rich and Wallace-Hadrill (1992). Roberts (1998) offers a more literary treatment of life in Athens.

A study of the relationship between festivals and communities can be read in Simon (1983) while details of life cycle rituals can be found in Demand (1994), Garland (1990, 1985) and Oakley and Sinos (1993). Images of city life are depicted in Berard (1991)

Family

The main examinations of the role of the family are Lacey (1968), Patterson (1998) and Pomeroy (1998). Demand (1994) and Golden (1990) give more specific considerations of the lives of children and new babies. Rawson (forthcoming 2010) is a collection of essays about different aspects of family life.

Economic Activity

A detailed study of ancient economics can be found in Austin and Vidal-Naquet (1977) and Gallant (1991), with Burford (1972) and Parkins and Smith (1998) giving more specific analyses of craftsmen and trade. Commercial behaviour is examined in Ault and Nevett (2005) and Kelly-Blazeby (2007). Examinations of the role of slaves in household and economy are made in Finley (1960) and Fisher (1994).

Gender and the Classical House

There is a range of studies that consider the role of women in society and in the house. Blundell (1995) gives a good general treatment of the role of women in society, as do the essays in Reeder (1995). Nevett (1995) and Walker (1983) offer specific views of the relationship between women and domestic architecture. Llewellyn-Jones (2003) puts forward the argument that women overcame social restrictions by veiling, and Davidson (1997) gives a picture of Athenian society from a male perspective, while the essays in Foxhall and Salmon (1998) offer a wider perspective of men in the ancient Greek world. Essays on the *symposium*, the male drinking party can be found in Murray (1990).

Religion

Studies of religion offer a range of different approaches from the role of the house in city festivals, seen in Bruit Zaidman and Schmitt Pantel (1992), to Vernant's (1983) work on the hearth and Yavis's (1949) examination of Greek altars. Details about practices in the domestic sphere can be found in Boedecker (2008), Burkert (1985), Faraone (2008), Morgan (2007a, 2007b) and Parker (2005). Douglas (1966) and Parker (1983) look at purification and include domestic rites, while more recent investigations into the hearth can be read in Foxhall (2008) and Tsakirgis (2008).

BIBLIOGRAPHY

Allison, P.M. (ed.), *The Archaeology of Household Activities* (London, 1999).

Ault, B.A., *The Excavations at Halieis. Vol. 2: The Houses: The Organisation and Use of Domestic Space* (Indianapolis, 2005).

Ault, B.A. and Nevett, L.C. (eds) *Ancient Greek Houses and Households: Chronological, Regional and Social Diversity* (Philadelphia, 2005).

Austin, M. and Vidal-Naquet, P., *Economic and Social History of Ancient Greece* (London, 1977).

Bagnall, R., *Reading Papyri, Writing Ancient History* (London and New York, 1995).

Bailey, D.W., *Prehistoric Figurines: Archaeologies of Representation and Corporeality* (London, 2005).

Beard, M. and Henderson, J., *Classical Art. From Greece to Rome* (Oxford, 2001).

Berard, C., *City of Images* (Princeton, 1991).

Bergquist, B., 'Sympotic Space: A Functional Aspect of Greek Dining Rooms', in O. Murray (ed.), *Sympotica. A Symposium on the Symposium* (Oxford, 1990), pp. 37–65.

Blundell, S., *Women in Ancient Greece* (London, 1995).

Boardman, J., 'Painted Funerary Plaques and Some Remarks on *Prothesis*', *Annual of the British School at Athens* 50 (1955) pp. 51–66.

Boedecker, D., 'Family Matters: Domestic Religion in Classical Greece', in J. Bodel and S.M. Olyan (eds), *Household and Family Religion in Antiquity* (Oxford, 2008), pp. 229–47.

Bognar, B., 'The Place of No-thingness. The Japanese House and the Oriental World Views of the Japanese', in J.P. Bourdier and N. Alsayyad (eds), *Dwellings, Settlement and Tradition: Cross-Cultural Perspectives* (New York and London, 1989), pp. 183–211.

Bookidis, N., 'Ritual Dining at Corinth', in N. Marinatos and R. Hägg (eds), *Greek Sanctuaries: New Approaches* (London, 1993), pp. 45–61.

Bookidis, N., Hansen, J., Snyder, L. and Goldberg, P., 'Dining in the Sanctuary of Demeter and Kore at Corinth', *Hesperia* 68 (1999), pp. 1–54.

Bookidis, N. and Stroud, R.S., *Corinth: Results of Excavations Conducted by the American School of Classical Studies at Athens. Vol.18 Pt.3: The Sanctuary of Demeter and Kore: Topography and Architecture* (Princeton, 1997).

Boyd, T.D. and Rudolph. W.W., 'Excavations at Porto Cheli and Vicinity. Preliminary Report IV: The Lower Town of Halieis, 1970–1977', *Hesperia* 47 (1978), pp. 333–55.

Bruit Zaidman, L. and Schmitt Pantel, P., *Religion in the Ancient Greek City*, trans. P. Cartledge (Cambridge and New York, 1992).

Burford, A., *Craftsmen in Greek and Roman Society* (London, 1972).

Burkert, W., *Greek Religion*, trans. J. Raffan (Oxford, 1985).

Cahill, N., *Household and City Organisation at Olynthus* (New Haven, CT, and London, 2002).

Camp, J.M., 'Excavations in the Athenian Agora: 1996 and 1997', *Hesperia* 68 (1999), pp. 255–83.

Camp, J.M., *The Archaeology of Athens* (New Haven, 2001).

Crawford, M. (ed), *Sources for Ancient History* (Cambridge, 1983).

Davidson, J., *Courtesans and Fishcakes. The Consuming Passions of Classical Athens* (London, 1997).

Davies, J.K., 'Society and Economy', in D.M. Lewis, J. Boardman, J.K. Davies, M. Ostwald (eds) *Cambridge Ancient History. Vol. V: The Fifth Century.* (Cambridge 1923; reprinted Cambridge, 1992), pp. 287–305.

Demand, N., *Birth, Death and Motherhood in Classical Athens* (Baltimore and London, 1994).

Dillon, M., *Girls and Women in Classical Greek Religion* (London, 2002).

Douglas, M., *Purity and Danger: An Analysis of Concepts of Pollution and Taboo* (London, 1966).

Faraone, C.A., 'Household Religion in Ancient Greece', in J. Bodel and S.M. Olyan (eds), *Household and Family Religion in Antiquity* (Oxford, 2008), pp. 210–28.

Finley, M.I., *Slavery in Classical Antiquity* (Cambridge, 1960).

Fisher, N.R.E., *Slavery in Classical Greece* (Bristol, 1994).

Foxhall, L., 'The Running Sands of Time: Archaeology and the Short Term', *World Archaeology* 31 (2000), pp. 484–98.

Foxhall, L., 'House Clearance: Unpacking the "Kitchen" in Classical Greece', in R.C. Westgate, N. Fisher and A.J.M. Whitley (eds), *Building*

Communities: House, Settlement and Society in the Aegean and Beyond (Athens, 2008), pp. 234–42.

Foxhall, L. and Salmon, J. (eds), *When Men Were Men: Masculinity, Power and Identity in Classical Antiquity* (London, 1998).

Gallant, T.W., *Risk and Survival in Ancient Greece. Reconstructing the Domestic Economy* (Cambridge, 1991).

Garland, R., *The Greek Way of Life* (New York, 1990; reprinted New York, 1993).

Garland, R., *The Greek Way of Death* (London, 1985; reprinted Bristol, 2001).

Golden, M., *Children and Childhood in Classical Athens* (Baltimore, 1990).

Graham, J.W., 'Olynthiaka 1-4', *Hesperia* 22 (1953), pp. 196–207.

Graham, J.W., 'Olynthiaka 5-6', *Hesperia* 23 (1954), pp. 320–46.

Graham, J.W., 'Origins and Interrelations of the Greek House and the Roman House', *Phoenix* 20 (1966), pp. 3–31.

Graham, J.W., 'Houses of Classical Athens', *Phoenix* 28 (1974), pp. 45–54.

Harrison, E.B., *The Athenian Agora XI: Archaic and Archaistic Sculpture* (Princeton, 1965).

Hedrick, C.W. Jr., *The Decrees of the Demotionidai*, American Classical Studies 22 (Atlanta, 1990).

Hoepfner., W. and Schwandner, E-L., *Haus und Stadt im klassischen Griechenland* (Munich, 1986; reprinted Munich, 1994).

Howgego, C., *Ancient History from Coins* (London and New York, 1995).

Jameson, M.H., 'Excavations at Porto Cheli and Vicinity. Preliminary Report I: Halieis, 1962–1968', *Hesperia* 38 (1969), pp. 311–42.

Jameson, M.H., 'Domestic Space in the Greek City-State', in S. Kent (ed.), *Domestic Architecture and the Use of Space* (Cambridge, 1990), pp. 92–113.

Jameson, M.H., 'The Asexuality of Dionysus', in T.H. Carpenter and C.A. Faraone (eds), *Masks of Dionysus* (London, 1993), pp. 45–64.

Jameson, M.H., 'Theoxenia', in R. Hägg (ed.), *Ancient Greek Cult Practice from the Epigraphical Evidence. Proceedings of the Second International Seminar on Ancient Greek Cult, Organised by the Swedish Institute at Athens, 22–24 Nov 1991* (Stockholm, 1994), pp. 35–57.

Jameson, M.H., 'A Hero-Cult at Halieis', in S. Bohm and K. von Eikstedt (eds), *Ithake: Festschrift für Jörg Schäfer zum 75 Geburtstag am 25. April 2001* (Würtzburg, 2001), pp. 197–202.

Jones, J.E., 'Town and Country Houses of Attica in Classical Times', in H. Mussche, P. Spitaels and F. Goemaere-De Poerk (eds), *Thorikos and* the Laurion in Archaic and Classical Times: Papers and Contributions of the Colloquim held in March 1973 at the State University of Ghent (Ghent, 1975), pp. 63–133.

Jones, J.E., Graham, A.J. and Sackett, L.H., 'An Attic Country House Below the Cave of Pan at Vari', Annual of the British School at Athens 68 (1973), pp. 355–452.

Kelly-Blazeby, C., 'The Archaeology of the Classical Greek Taverna/Wineshop', PhD thesis (Leicester, 2007).

Knigge, U., The Athenian Kerameikos: History, Monuments, Excavations, trans. by J. Binder (Athens, 1991).

Kovacscovics, W., Kerameikos XIV: Die Eckterrasse an der Gräberstrasse des Kerameikos (Berlin and New York, 1990).

Kramer, C., Village Ethnoarchaeology: Rural Iran in Perspective (New York, 1982).

Kurtz, D.C., Athenian White Lekythoi (Oxford, 1975).

Lacey, W.K., The Family in Classical Greece (London, 1968).

Lauter-Bufe, H. and Lauter, H., 'Wohnhäuser und Stadtviertel des Klassischen Athen', Mitteilungen des Deutschen Archäologischen Instituts, Athenische Abteilung 85/6 (1971), pp. 109–24.

Lawall, M., 'Graffiti, Wine Selling and the Re-Use of Amphoras in the Athenian Agora ca. 43–400 BC', Hesperia 69 (2000), pp. 3–90.

Leiwo, M., 'Religion or Other Reasons? Private Associations in Athens', in J. Frösén (ed.), Early Hellenistic Athens. Symptoms of a Change (Helsinki, 1997), pp. 103–17.

Lewis, S., The Athenian Woman: An Iconographic Handbook (London, 2002).

Llewellyn-Jones, L.J., Aphrodite's Tortoise. The Veiled Woman of Ancient Greece (London and Swansea, 2003).

McAllister, M.H., The Excavations at Ancient Halieis. Vol. 1: The Fortifications and Adjacent Structures (Indianapolis, 2005).

Morgan, J.E., 'Women, Religion and the Home', in D. Ogden (ed.), The Blackwell Companion to Greek Religion (Oxford, 2007a), pp. 297–310.

Morgan, J.E., 'Space and the Notion of a Final Frontier: Searching for Ritual Boundaries in the Classical Athenian Home', Kernos 20 (2007b), pp. 113–29.

Morris, I., 'Beyond Democracy and Empire: Athenian Art in Context', in D. Boedeker and K.A. Raaflaub (eds), Democracy, Empire and the Arts in Fifth Century Athens (Cambridge, MA, and London, 1998), pp. 59–86.

Murray, O. (ed.), Sympotica. A Symposium on the Symposium (Oxford, 1990).

Murray, O. and Price, S. (eds), *The Greek City from Homer to Alexander* (Oxford, 1990).

Neils, J. (ed.), *Goddess and Polis: The Panathenaic Festival in Ancient Athens* (Madison, 1992).

Nevett, L.C., *House and Society in the Ancient Greek World* (Cambridge, 1999).

Nevett, L.C., 'Gender Relations in the Classical Greek Household: The Archaeological Evidence', *Annual of the British School at Athens* 90 (1995), pp. 363–81.

Ogden, D. (ed.), *The Blackwell Companion to Greek Religion* (Oxford, 2007).

Oakley, J.H. and Sinos, R.H., *The Wedding in Ancient Athens* (Wisconsin, 1993).

Osborne, R., 'Social and Economic Implications of the Leasing of Land and Property in Classical and Hellenistic Greece', *Chiron* 18 (1988), pp. 279–323.

Osborne, R., 'The Economy and Trade', in J. Boardman (ed.), *Cambridge Ancient History: Plates to Vol. V and VI* (2nd edn, Cambridge, 1994), pp. 85–108.

Owens, E.J., *The City in the Greek and Roman World* (London, 1991).

Parker, R., *Miasma: Pollution and Purification in Early Greek Religion* (Oxford, 1983).

Parker, R., *Polytheism and Society at Athens* (Oxford, 2005).

Parkins, H. and Smith, C. (eds), *Trade, Traders and the Ancient City* (London, 1998).

Patterson, C.B., *The Family in Greek History* (Cambridge, MA, and London, 1998).

Pomeroy, S.B., *Families in Classical and Hellenistic Greece* (Oxford, 1998).

Rafn, B., 'Archaic and Classical Graves at Halieis: A Summary', in T. Fisher-Hansen, P. Guldager, J. Lund, M. Nielsen and A. Rathje (eds), *Recent Danish Research in Classical Archaeology*, Acta Hyperborea 3 (Copenhagen, 1991), pp. 57–71.

Rawson, B. (ed.), *A Companion to Families in the Greek and Roman Worlds* (Oxford, forthcoming 2010).

Reeder, E.D. (ed.), *Pandora. Women in Classical Greece* (Baltimore and Princeton, 1995).

Renfrew, C. and Bahn, P., *Archaeology: Theory, Methods and Practice* (London and New York, 1991; reprinted London and New York, 1995).

Rich, J. and Wallace-Hadrill, A. (eds), *City and Country in the Ancient World* (London, 1992).

Roberts, J., *City of Socrates* (London, 1998).

Robinson, D.M., 'A Preliminary Report on the Excavations at Olynthus', *American Journal of Archaeology* 33 (1929), pp. 53–76.

Robinson, D.M., *Excavations at Olynthus II: Architecture and Sculpture: Houses and Other Buildings* (Baltimore, 1930).

Robinson, D.M., 'The Residential Districts and the Cemeteries at Olynthus', *American Journal of Archaeology* 36 (1932), pp. 118–38.

Robinson, D.M., *Excavations at Olynthus V: Mosaics, Vases and Lamps of Olynthus Found in 1928 and 1931* (Baltimore, 1933).

Robinson, D.M., 'Inscriptions from Olynthus 1934', *Transactions of the American Philological Association* 65 (1934), pp. 103–37.

Robinson, D.M., *Excavations at Olynthus XII: Domestic and Public Architecture* (Baltimore, 1946).

Robinson, D.M., *Excavations at Olynthus XIII: Vases found in 1934 and 1938* (Baltimore, 1950).

Robinson, D.M. and Graham, A.J.W., *Excavations at Olynthus VIII: The Hellenic House* (Baltimore, 1938).

Scheffer, C., 'Gods on Athenian Vases: Their Function in the Archaic and Classical Periods', in C. Scheffer (ed.), *Ceramics in Context. Proceedings of the Internordic Colloquium on Ancient Pottery Held at Stockholm, 13–15 June 1997*, Studies in Classical Archaeology 12 (Stockholm, 2001), pp. 127–37.

Shanks, M., *Classical Archaeology of Greece: Experiences of the Discipline* (London, 1995).

Shapiro, H.A., 'The Iconography of Mourning in Athenian Art', *American Journal of Archaeology* 95 (1991), pp. 629–56.

Shear, T.L. Jr., 'The Athenian Agora: Excavations of 1971', *Hesperia* 42 (1973), pp. 123–79.

Simon, E., *Festivals of Attica* (Wisconsin, 1983).

Sparkes, B., 'The Greek Kitchen', *Journal of Hellenic Studies* 82 (1962), pp. 121–37.

Thompson, H.A., 'Activities in the Athenian Agora: 1958', *Hesperia* 28 (1959), pp. 91–108.

Thompson, H.A., 'Activities in the Athenian Agora: 1966–1967', *Hesperia* 37 (1968), pp. 36–72.

Thompson, H.A. and Wycherley, R.E., *The Athenian Agora XIV: The Agora of Athens. The History, Shape and Uses of an Ancient City Centre* (Princeton, 1972).

Tomlinson, R.A., 'Two Buildings in the Sanctuary of Asklepios', *Journal of Hellenic Studies* 89 (1969), pp. 106–17.

Tomlinson, R.A., From Mycenae to Constantinople: The Evolution of the Ancient City (London, New York, 1992).

Travlos, J., *Pictorial Dictionary of Ancient Athens* (London, 1971).

Tsakirgis, B., 'Fire and Smoke: Hearths, Braziers and Chimneys in the Greek House', in R.C. Westgate, N. Fisher and A.J.M. Whitley (eds), *Building Communities: House, Settlement and Society in the Aegean and Beyond* (Athens, 2008), pp. 225–31.

Vernant, J-P., 'Hestia-Hermes: The Religious Expression of Space and Movement in Ancient Greece', in J-P. Vernant, *Myth and Thought Among the Greeks* (London, 1983), pp. 127–75.

Walker, S., 'Women and Housing in Classical Greece: The Archaeological Evidence', in A. Cameron and A. Kuhrt (eds), *Images of Women in Antiquity* (London, 1983), pp. 81–92.

Whitley, J., *The Archaeology of Ancient Greece* (Cambridge, 2001).

Wilkins, J., *The Boastful Chef. The Discourse of Food in Ancient Greek Comedy* (Oxford, 2000).

Williams II, C.K., 'The City of Corinth and its Domestic Religion', *Hesperia* 50 (1981), pp. 408–21.

Wycherley, R.E., *How the Greeks Built Cities* (London, 1962).

Yavis, C.G., *Greek Altars* (Missouri, 1949).

Young, R.S., 'An Industrial District of Ancient Athens', *Hesperia* 20 (1951), pp. 135–250.

INDEX

GREECE AND ROME LIVE

Also available in this series:

Ancient Greece in Film and Popular Culture, Gideon Nisbet (2006; second edition 2008)

Ancient Rome at the Cinema: Story and Spectacle in Hollywood and Rome, Elena Theodorakopoulos (2010)

Augustine: The Confessions, Gillian Clark (2005)

Augustus, First Roman Emperor: Power, Propaganda and the Politics of Survival, Matthew D.H. Clark (2010)

Greek Tyranny, Sian Lewis (2009)

Gruesome Deaths and Celibate Lives: Christian Martyrs and Ascetics, Aideen M. Hartney (2005)

Hadrian's Wall and its People, Geraint Osborn (2006)

Hannibal: Rome's Greatest Enemy, Dexter Hoyos (2008)

Julius Caesar, Robert Garland (2004)

The Politics of Greek Tragedy, David M. Carter (2007)

Reading Catullus, John Godwin (2008)

The Tragedies of Sophocles, James Morwood (2008)

Forthcoming titles:

After Virgil: The Poetry, Politics and Perversion of Roman Epic, Robert Cowan

The Law in Ancient Greece, Christopher Carey

Pausanias: An Ancient Guide to Greece, John Taylor

The Trojan War, Emma Stafford